IMPROVISING

IMPROVISING

How to Master the Art

Gerre Hancock

OXFORD UNIVERSITY PRESS

New York   Oxford

1994

OXFORD UNIVERSITY PRESS

Oxford   New York
Athens   Auckland   Bangkok   Bombay
Calcutta   Cape Town   Dar es Salaam   Delhi
Florence   Hong Kong   Istanbul   Karachi
Kuala Lumpur   Madras   Madrid   Melbourne
Mexico City   Nairobi   Paris   Singapore
Taipei   Tokyo   Toronto

and associated companies in
Berlin   Ibadan

Published by Oxford University Press, Inc.,
198 Madison Avenue, New York, New York   10016-4314

Oxford is a registered trademark of Oxford University Press

Library of Congress Cataloging-in-Publication Data

Hancock, Gerre, 1934–
Improvising: how to master the art / Gerre Hancock.
p.   cm. Includes bibliographical references.
ISBN 0-19-385881-9
1. Improvisation (Music) 2. Organ—Instruction and study.
I. Title.
MT191.I5H36 1994
786.5' 136—dc20   94-11482
CIP
MN

9 8 7 6 5 4 3

Printed in the United States of America
on acid-free paper

Contents

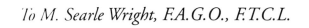
To M. Searle Wright, F.A.G.O., F.T.C.L.

Introduction

Why learn to improvise?

In order to play the works of other composers which are improvisatory in nature with more conviction and authority? Certainly: one thinks at once of the keyboard works of Titelouze, de Grigny, Buxtehude, Böhm, Bach, Beethoven, Franck, Dupré, Messiaen, and Cage, to mention but a few. Many of their works actually began as improvisations, because these composers possessed renowned improvisatory prowess.

In order to perform the music for divine service with greater flexibility and versatility? Of course: the various liturgies and services of many denominations seem to beg for improvisations, both brief and extended, that will enrich these ceremonies and give continuity to the flow and drama inherent in them. Such liturgical and even extra-liturgical occasions demand the flexibility that only skilled and imaginative improvisation can provide.

This is all very sound, and certainly affords ample justification for learning and mastering this neglected art, but the chief reason to learn improvisation is simply that our musical personalities are incomplete and underdeveloped if we are unable to express ourselves in a spontaneous fashion. The ability to improvise is central to our musicianship; without it, musicians are simply not "compleat."

Not surprisingly, many musicians are discouraged from attempting to improvise because of a mythical aura of mystery surrounding the art; they perceive it as a special endowment bestowed on only a chosen few and unattainable by the rest. The plain truth is that all musicians are capable of splendid improvisation, be it modest or grand. As in any other art, improvising must be analyzed, planned, and practiced both in private and in public, the more carefully, systematically, and conscientiously, the better.*

Although I seek in this book to suggest ways and means of practicing improvising, I make no pretense at providing either the definitive word or a learned treatise on this great art, such as Marcel Dupré has already given us in his *Cours complet d'improvisation à l'orgue*. In this work, which cannot be too highly praised, Dupré's approach is thorough, his method logical, his teaching inspired. My book is intended instead to serve as an informal workbook, a compendium of very basic ideas that will point the musician in the proper direction on the road to the mastery of improvisation. The approach remains the same in each chapter: (1) analyze the form of a model piece

---

* Here a contradiction seems to confront the musician: how can improvised music be spontaneous if it has been practiced beforehand? The answer is simply that if we must practice the notated music of other composers in order to perform it properly, all the more do we need to practice our own music, even if not previously written down.

from the works of a favorite composer; (2) write out your own adaptation in both musical and non-musical outlines; and (3) practice on the keyboard what you have written down. Improvisation is, in the end, another way of composing music.

I have planned the book in such a way that I hope its ideas will be accessible to all musicians, even those with a modest amount of formal musical education in matters of theory, harmony, counterpoint, form and analysis, and composition. To this end, the language used is deliberately simplified—indeed, over-simplified. But all the ideas suggested here may be elaborated upon and extended to levels of great subtlety and sophistication.

It is hoped that the methods suggested here may be of use not only to the individual, but also to a group in a classroom or workshop under the supervision of an expert coach or teacher. In the end, improvisation cannot really be taught, but only suggested. The musician becomes her or his own teacher using the processes suggested in this book. Moreover, all keyboard players, not merely organists, can benefit from these ideas.

The most troubling obstacles in learning to improvise will stem most probably from our inhibitions. The challenge of destroying these inhibitions becomes liberating and satisfying, making possible self-expression through improvising that becomes deeply fulfilling.

Libraries abound with books by great teachers who, like Dupré, thus allow us to study with them. The books suggested in the Bibliography are but a few among many that are available; they are included because of my own experience and success in consulting them and in commending them to others, who have likewise found them helpful.

Study the works of as many composers as you possibly can. Explore keyboard literature, to be sure, but travel farther, into the realms of symphonic, operatic, vocal, choral, chamber-music, theater, jazz, and rock literature. If it is true, as the old adage says, that we are composites of all whom we have met, then we must certainly apply this truth to our musical selves.

If you perceive that your improvised music-making is trite (what, in fact, is "trite" music, anyway?) or that it sounds like another composer, then rejoice: you are launched as an improviser, you have made the all-important first step, and your dissatisfaction will spur you on to search for and discover your own distinct and unique musical personality. Some years ago, a gifted and conscientious student said to me, "I am so discouraged; every time I improvise, I sound just like Fauré." More impressed than amused by her predicament, I replied, "Be grateful that you sound like that great composer. In fact, would you please teach us all how to sound just like Fauré?" Just as we first learn our native language as infants by imitation, so, too, do we learn our musical language by imitation, however unconscious the process may be. In fact, a deliberate effort to mimic another composer can be a surprisingly instructive experience.

Perhaps the most formidable problem of all is not *what* we say but *how* we go about saying it. Here is perhaps the most important goal of this book: to help the improviser organize his or her ideas by means of a systematic plan. The most important step is learning to determine the required space and using no less and no more than that. I had the great privilege of studying improvisation with Nadia Boulanger in Paris. At the first lesson, I was asked to improvise on a theme of Mlle. Boulanger's choosing, using a simple ABA song form. The A section, of some twenty-four measures' length, went fairly well, as did the B section, of some sixteen measures' length and built upon an inversion of the A theme. With confidence thus renewed I began to elaborate at greater length, traveling to one key for a diminution of the A theme, back to the tonic for an augmentation of the B theme, changing to yet another key for a diminution over an augmentation, and so forth, each scheme growing in ambition and ornateness. All considerations of time and space were consequently forgotten as the young performer continued to show off, to put it bluntly. After a while, a tap on my shoulder brought the organ playing to an abrupt halt, and Mlle. Boulanger asked this simple question: "Why do you keep playing the organ when the piece was finished some time ago?" After all these years, the great lesson I learned then is as fresh as though I had learned it only yesterday; the considerations of space, balance, and proportion are essential in creating any work of art.

Two axioms might be applied to the art of improvising. The first is, *Never stop.* Accidents will inevitably happen; if and when they do, keep playing, even if it is only a trill. For example, suppose you are improvising a lovely duo when suddenly an unexpected and harsh dissonance occurs, as in measure 4 below:

Make the most of it; don't stop; simply continue the duo as before, making sure to repeat the "mistake." Thus is balance in form realized, even if unexpectedly:

The second axiom is, *Salvation is never more than half a step away.* Note in the above example that the dissonance in measure 3 vanishes with ease when each of the two voices is moved apart by only a half step.

A useful way to practice improvising without stopping is to play, in one hand at a time, a long series of stepwise notes without rests; begin with whole notes, then half notes, then quarter notes, eighths, sixteenths, thirty-seconds, and so on. When each hand has mastered this simple but essential technique, practice hands together in the same manner. The rhythmic outline might look somewhat like this:

The chief goal is to develop the ability to keep the hands on the keyboard, regardless of circumstances that might distract the improviser. This exercise is primarily digital in nature; if some music-making begins to emerge (and it will, in time), so much the better!

Above all, remember that you are the creator and the artist; we are your audience. What might sound "wrong" to you might sound beautiful to us! In any case, your performance of your improvisation is the only authentic one, the first and the last.

I am in awe of and enormously grateful for the invaluable guidance, help, patience, and encouragement of Susan Brailove, Manager of the Music Department at Oxford University Press in New York, and her colleague Paul Schlotthauer, Associate Editor, without whose confidence and attention to detail and clarity this book would never have existed. I would also like to thank Clifford G. Richter, music editor, and Steven Powell, compositor, for their consummate skill in making the musical language speak clearly from the printed page. My gratitude and admiration go to all these friends who never stopped in assuring this book's salvation, step by step.

I have been extraordinarily fortunate in being able to study the art of improvisation with Mlle. Boulanger and M. Searle Wright. Much of what is found in these pages comes from their example, wisdom, and encouragement. I remain, with profound gratitude, ever in their debt.

New York   G. H.
March 1994

IMPROVISING

1. The Scale

The musician should feel comfortably at home in all major and minor keys and in most if not all traditional church modes. Clearly, an intimate knowledge of each key and how closely or distantly it is related to all the others is of prime importance to the improviser.

A systematic method of practicing will produce fluency and ease in all keys. Here are suggestions for practicing to achieve these goals, which may be practiced on both manual and pedal keyboards. In fact, feel free to use the pedal keyboard from the very beginning, even if you feel that your pedal technique is limited. The idea is to use as much of your technique as possible from the beginning. This will give you the advantage and opportunity of expanding your technique through improvising, and, further, of improvising more expansively through the technique thereby acquired.

1. Create a melody utilizing the scale exclusively. Limit yourself to one octave, beginning with the tonic note, playing up or down that octave, and returning to the note of origin. Think of the scale as a tune, using differing note values to give it character. Limit yourself at all times to a specific number of measures, thus defining the space for your improvising. The following examples are limited to eight measures.

Note that each example has some degree of rhythmic symmetry, giving it shape and contour. In the beginning stages, don't permit yourself a skip or a repeated note within the scale; if you do, focus will be placed upon the intervallic relationships between notes. Practice these one-voice scales with the express purpose of creating, within these limitations, an attractive melody. Remember the importance of space, whatever the specific number of measures you might choose for each scale.

Next, without changing the key signature, practice scales in the relative minor key.

Note that we are experimenting with different time signatures. There are no skips or leaps, and each scale is first practiced either by descending and then ascending, or vice versa. Such a system of practice enables the improviser to re-think the same scale as a different tune, and to benefit from and enjoy the variety that results from the alternating directions of scale movement. Care has been taken to give a specific character to each improvisation by means of tempo, dynamics, and phrase markings.

2. Create a scale melody as before, but add another voice. Here the scale should be practiced as the melody in either the top or the bottom voice. If the scale is in the top voice, think of the bottom voice as the bass part; if the scale is in the bottom voice, think of the top voice as a descant or obbligato of an imitative or free nature. Again, allow yourself the discipline of a predetermined number of measures, and make the creation of expressive music your primary goal.

At this point we begin to establish an organized means of practicing the improvisation of and on the scales. Examples 1–4 are in the key of C major; Examples 5–8 are in its relative minor key. We now set a pattern by moving a perfect fifth away from C major and A minor to the keys of G major and E minor, respectively. From here on, you are encouraged to practice these examples by playing as often as desired the bass parts on the pedal keyboard, varying the pitches from 8' to 16' or 4', singly or in combinations. Here is another opportunity to open the ear to possibilities of tonal range and color.

Example 9

Example 10

scale with added, repeated notes

Example 11

scale with added, repeated notes

Example 12

Example 13

Example 14

Andante

scale

mf

scale with added, repeated notes

Example 15

Adagio

pp

scale

cresc.

dim.

Example 16

Allegretto

f scale with added, repeated notes

scale

Note that effort is made to vary the direction, time signature, style, and mood of each scale, and that we have not yet gone beyond the natural form of the minor scale; melodic and harmonic versions will require small adjustments.

You will want to play two versions of each scale, in which the scale is practiced in one voice, beginning with an ascent, and again in the same voice, beginning with a descent; then repeat this procedure for the same scale as it appears in the other voice. In our examples, note that each scale does not necessarily begin on the first beat of the measure, or even on one of its strong beats. To extend one's flexibility and imagination in improvising is ever-important; stretching toward and through variety replaces potential tedium with fresh challenge and discovery.

3. Create a scale melody as before, but add a third voice. Here the scale will appear in the top, middle, and bottom voices. We will remain within the space of eight measures, always remembering that the "main event," the scale, should be thought of as an appealing melody.

Continuing our pattern, we proceed with our traversal of the circle of fifths, now moving to D major, with two versions (Exx. 18 and 19) of the scale in the middle voice ascending and descending:

Example 17

Example 18

Example 19

Example 20

We now follow the same procedure in B minor:*

Example 21

Example 22

Example 23

*Note that we have not, in the interest of space, practiced two versions each of the top and bottom voices, as we did previously. The improviser should do so, nonetheless, in order to control and master the art of improvising in three-part textures.

Example 24

4. *Create a scale melody as before, but add a fourth voice.* Here the scales will be found in the soprano, alto, tenor, and bass voices. We will now begin to vary the number of measures for each improvisation, having by now mastered the eight-measure format. We continue our pattern of moving around the circle of fifths. The interior voices will each be illustrated twice, as in the preceding examples, one beginning with a descent in the alto (Ex. 26) and the next beginning with an ascent in the same voice. The tenor scales will be treated in the same fashion. We now move to A major:

Example 25

Example 26

Example 27

Example 28

Example 29

We continue the pattern by moving to the relative key of F♯ minor. We will vary the number of measures, as before, and practice the three forms of the minor scale (natural, melodic, and harmonic):

Example 31

Example 32

Example 33

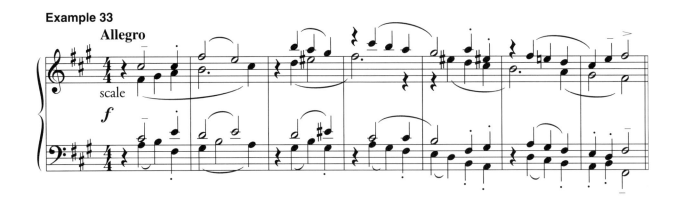

Example 34

Example 35

Example 36

Note that, again, there are not written examples of both ascent- and descent-beginning scales for the soprano and bass voices (as there were in the two-voice improvisations); it is assumed that the improviser will practice two versions of each scale voice within each key.

The modes provide colorful and interesting means of practicing in this method. In the beginning, you may want to confine yourself to playing only on the white keys, avoiding all accidentals, so that you can savor the unique qualities of each mode. For example, improvisations in the Dorian mode would stretch from D to D, the Phrygian from E to E, and the other modes accordingly. Here is a three-voice improvisation in the Mixolydian mode:

Example 37
Andante

Having worked without any repeated notes or any skips within the scale, we may now begin to improvise scale melodies that invite and accommodate them. Additionally, embellishments will naturally suggest themselves in the process. In fact, the result may be difficult for the listener to discern as a scale, for it is now the barest foundation upon which the improvisation is built. We now proceed to E major:

Example 38
Largo

You should have little difficulty—and much pleasure—in extending your abilities to improvise on the diatonic scale and the chromatic scale. The approach, in terms of ensuring the integrity and independence of each voice, should be the same. Remember to respect the amount of space you plan to use.

Here is an example of the diatonic or whole-tone scale improvised on C♯:

Example 39

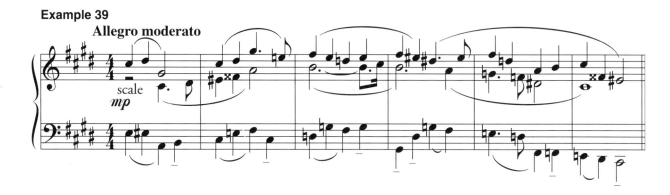

Here is an example of a chromatic scale improvised on C♯:

Example 40

Franck and maybe even Reger would blush!

In all these exercises we have avoided the concept of "harmonizing the scale." Certainly, traditional harmonizing approaches to the scale are important, especially in giving us an understanding of each key. Still, our purpose here has been to create a sense of freedom, uninhibited by the strictures of the "rules," however valid they may be. Our goal is simply to achieve a very personal means of self-expression, a goal for which these exercises are designed. To this end, note the many choices we have made in terms of time signature, tempo, dynamic marking, style, and mood. The improviser's distinct musical personality will consequently begin to emerge and evolve.

At the same time, we need to realize that these "rules" of harmony and counterpoint, as they have evolved through centuries of Western musical creativity, give us the foundation upon which to build and develop our improvisations. Thus we should begin our quest armed with as much traditional harmonic equipment as our study of theory will permit. Such a grounding gives us the freedom to experiment and extend through that learned discipline into wider fields of harmonic trial and error. This eventually enables us to discover our own individual harmonic language and style.

As the ultimate model, we look to the harmonic vocabulary of the mid-eighteenth century, the epicenter of harmony as the support and enhancement of melody, and often referred to by musicians as the Common Practice Period. This style has been eloquently taught by such composer/teachers as Walter Piston (see the Bibliography). If we are conversant with the rules by which such harmonizations were achieved, we will then be able to break those rules, conscious that we are doing so and why.

For instance, in eighteenth-century style, certain consecutive intervals are avoided, considered in poor taste, if not actually "wrong": consecutive seconds, fifths, and sevenths are forbidden as aurally offensive or simply uninteresting. Voice-leading is also of paramount importance in this style, given the inherent contrapuntal nature of each individual voice.

Here is an example of the manner in which a pupil of Bach might have harmonized a scalewise melody:

Example 41

Here is the manner in which we might harmonize that melody today, aware that our divergence from the rules grows out of an urge to find alternative color and style. Being mindful of those rules both informs and liberates our efforts to seek out our individual harmonic language.

Example 42

Moderato

This example is resplendent with consecutive fifths, awkward voice-leading, improper intervallic leaps, unprepared dissonances, monotonous chromatic movement, unrelated triads, and other stylistic incongruities. Even so, this harmonization proceeds basically from its eighteenth-century precedents. The best improvising is based upon a solid foundation of harmony.

Note how well scales, in either parallel or contrary motion, work in support of each other.

Not all voices of a given scale are necessarily active at all times; in fact, more interest is created if they play off each other, and are occasionally silent.

You need not keep the same time signature within the space of an improvisation (Exx. 11 and 21).

Above all, think of and approach each scale as if you are improvising a piece of music, however brief it might be. Never waste an opportunity to create something wonderfully musical. Don't be concerned if what you produce sounds "trite" or like "someone else's music" to the listener; the music is yours and yours alone and therefore unique. After all, very few musicians, whether improvising or composing on paper, have consistently created genuine masterpieces at each effort.

We have dwelt at length on scale improvisations simply because they are fundamental to all the following forms of improvising that we will be attempting. You are urged to master them thoroughly.

Recommendations

1. Write out, away from the keyboard, examples of what you will be improvising at the keyboard, and then try them out at the keyboard. What you have noted down may not always sound as you intended. By first committing what you want to improvise to staff paper, and then really hearing it, you will have accomplished the largest part of creating the music that you will be improvising.

2. Practice the first half of each example in this chapter and supply your own improvisation for the second half, so that you have the experience of completing a musical thought. Play from the printed examples up to a certain pre-determined point, and then refrain from looking at the printed page while you improvise a conclusion. Make sure that the same style is maintained, so that your completion is a logical relation and conclusion to what has gone before.

3. When you are improvising in virtually any form, count aloud so that you may monitor the number of measures and the amount of time you have chosen. In each measure, count the first beats strongly, numbering the measures as they transpire. For example, in $\frac{3}{4}$ time, count aloud: *1–2–3, 2–2–3, 3–2–3, 4–2–3*, and so on. A welcome dividend is that your sense of space and form will be enhanced, not only in your own music-making, but also in perceiving the formal structures of music by others as well.

4. Don't feel confined to conventional time signatures. In several examples we have noted oft-changing time signatures. These are, however, purely optional and need not be taken as the only guides.

5. Here is a suggested day-by-day practice schedule, providing a weekly regimen. As in all art, consistent and regular practice is vitally important.

WEEK 1:   C major

Day	Number of voices	Scale in soprano (ascent and descent)	Scale in middle (ascent and descent)	Scale in tenor (ascent and descent)	Scale in bass (ascent and descent)
1	1	Twice each	Twice each	Twice each	Twice each
	2	Twice each	—	—	Twice each
2	3	Twice each	Twice each	—	Twice each
3	4	Twice each	—	—	Twice each
4	4	Twice each	Twice each	—	Twice each
5	4	Twice each	—	Twice each	Twice each
6	4	Twice each	Twice each	Twice each	Twice each

WEEK 2:   A minor. As above, adding melodic versions of the scale on Day 4, harmonic versions on Day 5, and all three in varying combinations on Day 6.

WEEK 3:   G major. As Week 1 above.

WEEK 4:   E minor. As Week 2 above.

Obviously these schemes may contract or expand, depending on your maximum work habits, and depending on whether you add a seventh day, omitted here. With or without it, however, you should become a well-tempered improviser within approximately forty-eight weeks.

2. The Phrase

The musical phrase is the fundamental and essential foundation upon which most music is created, whether the music is a song or a fugue, whether homophonic or contrapuntal. Being able to improvise on other composers' phrases is as important as being able to improvise on one's own. In any case, the improviser creates phrases whenever she or he improvises. Remember our improvisations built around the scales, which then became, in their own way, phrases themselves.

We will begin with the very simplest kind of phrases. At the risk of over-simplifying our terminology, we will call them "questions and answers." As with the scales, we will work at first in eight-measure phrases, each consisting of two four-measure units: a four-measure question followed by a four-measure answer. The answer, as a resolution to the question, will not only relate to the question but will become a sort of thematic and rhythmic twin to it as well.

Here is a question that receives a totally unrelated answer:

Example 1

Here the same question receives an appropriate and satisfying answer:

Example 2

1. Create phrases by improvising answers to the following questions. In the beginning, be arbitrary: the length of the answer should be exactly equal to the length of the question, and the answer should be truly a resolution to the question through close rhythmic, thematic, and stylistic relationships. The concept is one of complete balance.

As in the practicing of scales, we will begin with one-voice improvisations. Interesting is the vast amount of literature for one-voice [monophonic] music; consider, for instance, the perfection of Gregorian chants or the charms of folk songs. There are ample precedents in keyboard literature alone for improvising with only one voice. The answers, in this beginning stage, should end on the tonic note, simply to avoid any possible ambiguity of key.

Example 3

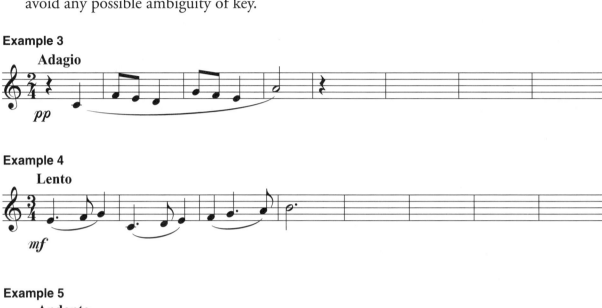

Example 4

Example 5

Example 6

Example 7

Example 8

Example 9

Example 10

Note that each question is capable of receiving at least two answers within its key signature: one in C major and another in A minor. You will want to improvise as many answers as you can at each practice session.

We might reverse our procedure at this point and improvise the questions, taking our clues from the answers written before us. The improviser often works on this premise, especially when improvising on the themes of others.

Example 11

Example 12

2. *Create phrases by improvising answers to the following questions in two voices.* We resume our practice scheme of moving around the circle of fifths. To vary this routine, let us change our direction, moving backward to keys which have flats in their key signatures. Thus we find ourselves in F major. Remember that to maintain the contour and style of either question or answer when improvising its counterpart, the bottom voice should be considered the bass when the phrase is in the treble clef, and the top voice a descant and/or imitative voice when the phrase is in the bass clef.

Example 13

Example 14

Example 15

Example 16

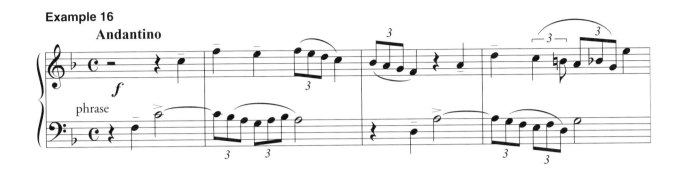

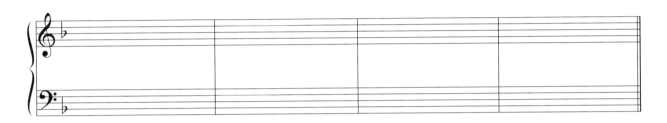

As before, we use different time signatures, tempi, styles, and moods. The phrase, the "main event," appears alternately in the treble and bass clefs. Now we move to D minor.

Example 17

Example 18

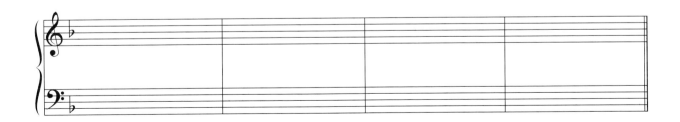

Example 19
Allegro molto

Example 20
Moderato

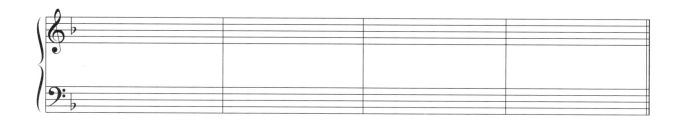

Be sure to practice answers using all three forms of the minor scale.

    3. Create phrases by improvising answers to the following questions in three voices. Here the phrase will be found in the top, middle, and bottom voices. We move to B♭ major:

Example 21
Andante

Example 22

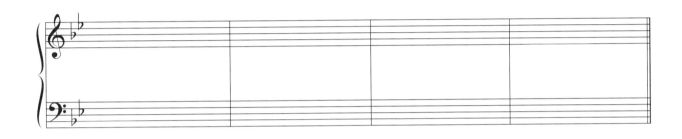

Example 23

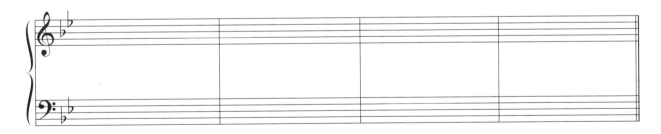

Example 24

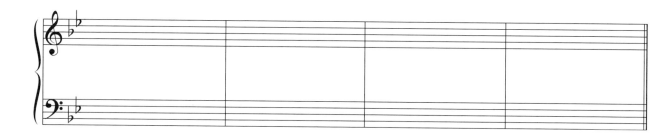

and to G minor:

Example 25

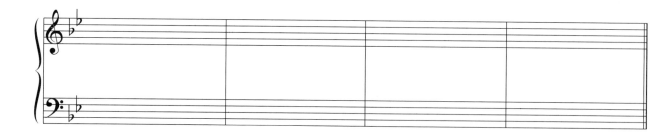

Example 26

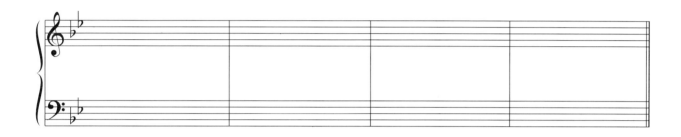

Example 27

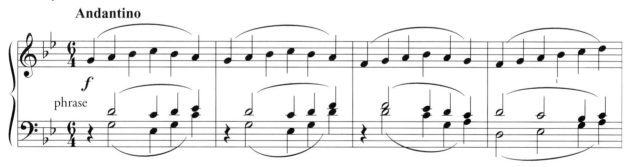

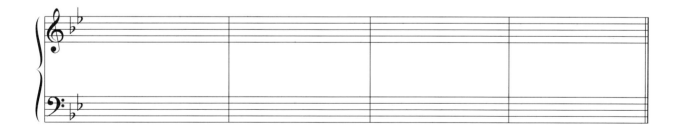

Example 28

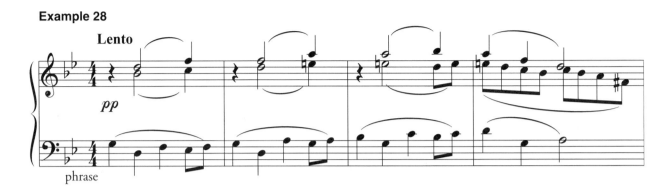

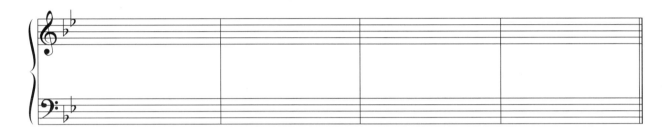

Again, space limitations require that we not supply written examples for answers to questions in the top and bottom voices (as we did for the two-voice improvisations). You will nonetheless want to practice playing several answers for each question in each of the three voices.

    4. Create phrases by improvising answers to the following questions in four voices. Here the phrase will be found successively in the soprano, alto, tenor, and bass voices. We will now begin to vary the number of measures for each improvisation, having by now mastered the eight-measure format. The interior voices will be illustrated twice, as in each of the preceding phrases. We move to E♭ major:

Example 29

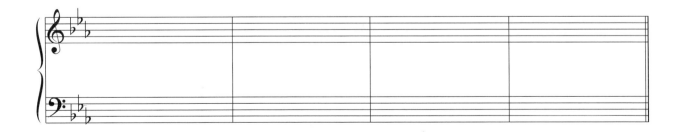

Example 30

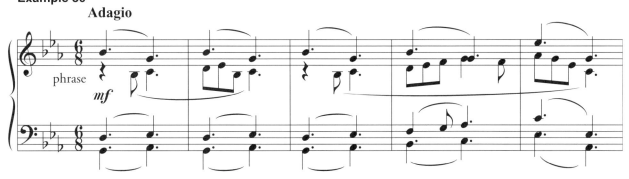

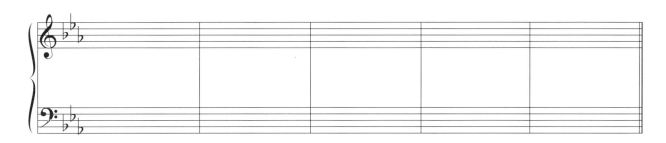

Example 31

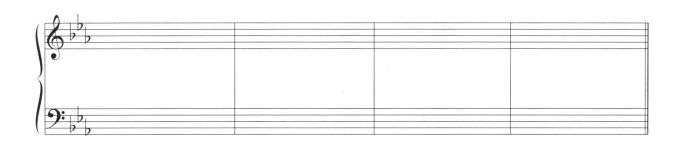

Example 32

Moderato

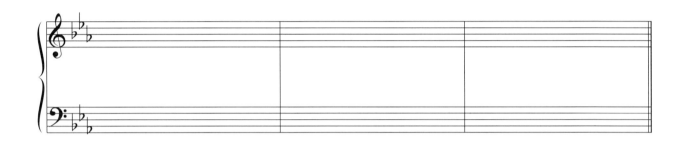

Example 33

Andante

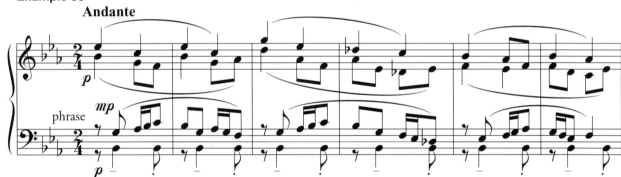

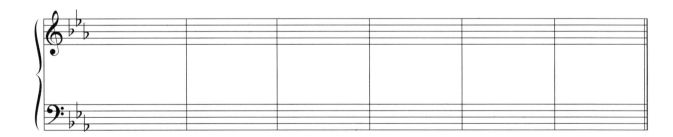

Example 34

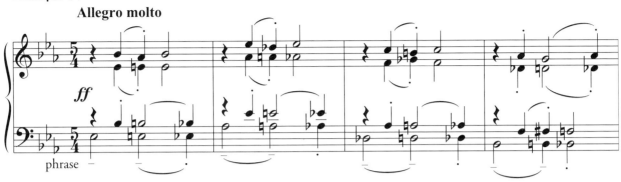

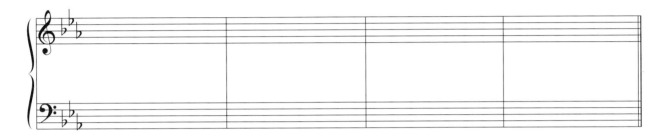

and to C minor:

Example 35

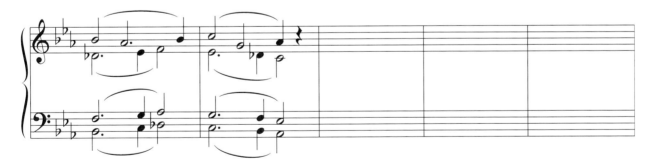

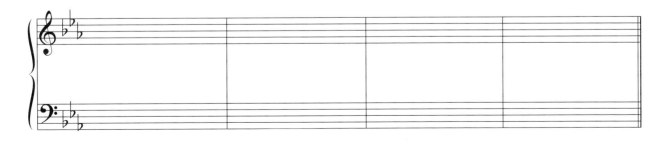

Example 36

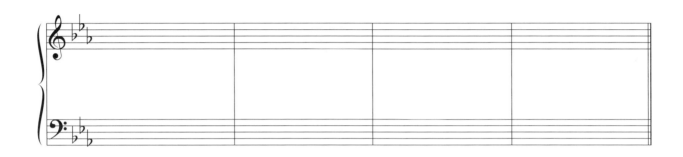

Example 37

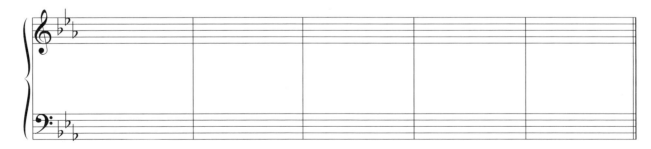

Example 38

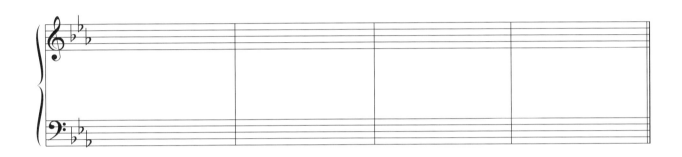

Example 39

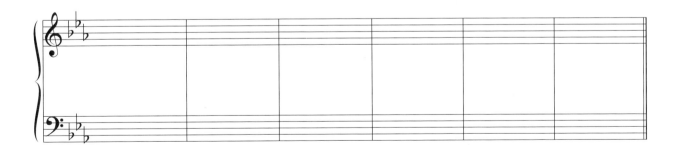

Example 40

You will want to practice at least two versions of those examples where the phrases are in the soprano and bass voices.

We should not by any means confine ourselves to the standard major and minor keys, but should improvise in the modes as well. As with the scale improvisations, you may want, in the initial stages, to play only on the white keys. Here is a two-voice question in the Dorian mode (the answer should end on D):

Example 41

a three-voice question in the Phrygian mode (the answer should end on E):

Example 42

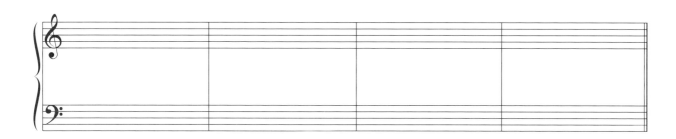

and a four-voice question in the Lydian mode (the answer should end on F):

Example 43

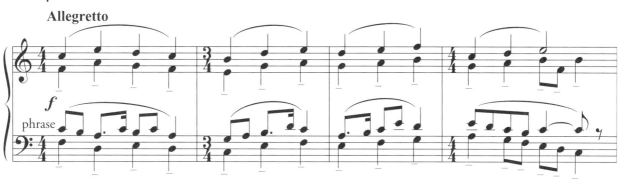

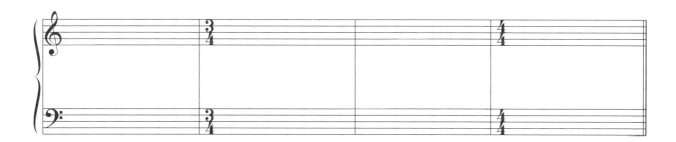

Our treatment of these phrases has not necessarily resulted in "harmonization" of the melodies, but rather are attempts to make musical statements by essaying varying styles in a rather free manner. A chief goal is the development of each improviser's personal means of self-expression.

In most examples, all voices are not employed in every beat throughout the improvisation; textural contrasts thus begin to emerge.

The time signatures may vary within even a short improvisation, but the symmetry and space remain constant and balanced (see Exx. 40 and 43).

Again, our practicing is far more than a mere set of exercises; above all, we should think of every improvisation as a piece of music, however brief and simple it may be. Never waste an opportunity to create something musically beautiful.

We have dwelt at length on improvising phrases, questions, and answers because they are so fundamentally important in constructing the form and context of the music we shall be improvising in the following pages. Utter mastery of phrase-creating is therefore of the greatest importance.

Recommendations

1. Write out, away from the keyboard, examples of your answers to each of the above questions that you will be improvising, making sure that you check what you have written at the keyboard. Practice as many different answers for each question as you are able before going on to the next example.

2. Write out your *own* questions and improvise their answers; then reverse the process, writing out the answers and improvising the questions.

3. If you feel occasional need for developing independence of voices, try employing parallel intervals, especially parallel thirds and sixths, which are the most consonant. Then try parallel fourths and fifths, which are very colorful, and then parallel seconds and sevenths, which are dissonant without necessarily being too jarring. Here are some examples, using the same tune, for which you may keep the same fixed intervals in improvising the answers (don't be alarmed by the occasional "surprise" you may hear):

Example 44 (consecutive thirds)

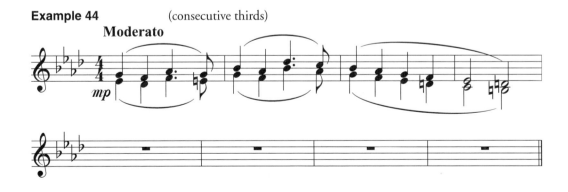

Example 45 (consecutive sixths)

Example 46 (consecutive fourths)

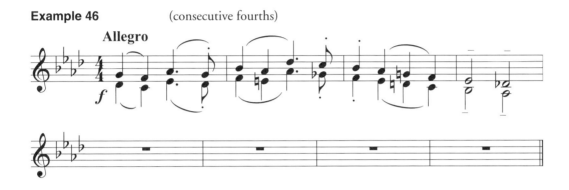

Example 47 (consecutive fifths)

Example 48 (consecutive seconds)

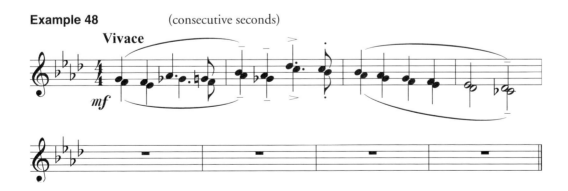

Example 49 (consecutive sevenths)

These parallel intervals may move by either whole or half steps, or combinations of both, in one voice or in both simultaneously. In determining which choice to make, we should think both vertically and horizontally. In the vertical relationships between the voices, we may choose major or minor, augmented or diminished intervals. These choices will be made with regard to the horizontal relationships, where a sense of line for each of the two voices will ultimately lead us to determine which of the two steps, with their resulting intervals, to choose for each improvisation. Once more we realize that our chief goal is to create a satisfying musical statement.

We will want to practice these examples and their intervals in inverted configurations. Here are three examples:

Example 50 (example 47 inverted)

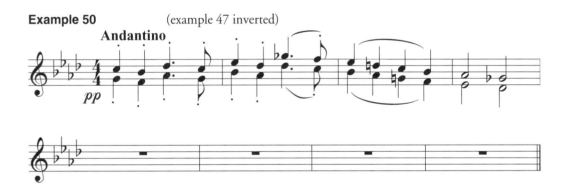

Example 51 (example 48 inverted)

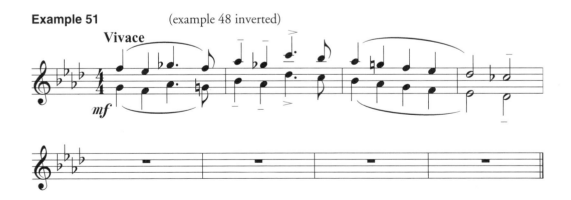

Example 52 (example 49 inverted)

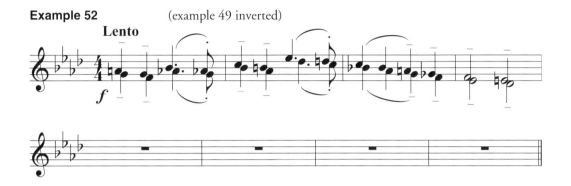

Some striking sonorities may evolve when certain parallel intervals are applied in varying combinations. Don't be inhibited about experimenting with any number and combination of consecutive intervals:

Example 53

As for giving organization and energy to the bass line, practice constantly moving scale-based patterns in duplet, triplet, and quadruplet groups:

Example 54

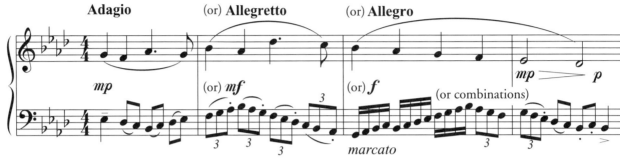

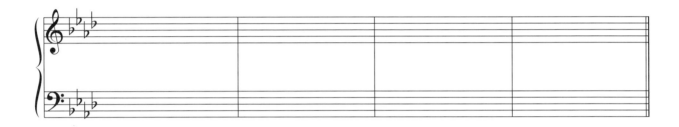

Ostinato-like patterns are also a possibility:

Example 55

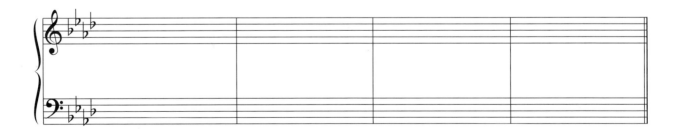

You will want to practice the questions and answers with one of the above three bass-clef options at a time (Exx. 53–55); then invent your own figurations, alone and in combination. Practicing inversions of these voices will give you ideas for other voices.

Example 56

The possibilities of combining the use of parallel intervals and the bass lines just illustrated will give you an almost infinite range of choices from which to practice.

As in the learning of all keyboard literature, very slow practice is strongly recommended. Also valuable is practice by each hand alone, especially in developing the manual dexterity necessary to execute these improvisations. Equally important is the practice of the pedals alone, then pedals with each hand, and ultimately feet and hands together.

4.   Practice answers to each question posed here in its relative major/minor key. For example, practice answers in C minor for questions in E♭ major; practice answers in E♭ major for questions in C minor. This will give you increased ability to improvise transitions and modulations later on.

5.   Just as the number of measures is carefully controlled, so the individual ranges of each voice, especially when that voice is the phrase, should be carefully controlled. A composer of a choral work would not allow the voices to exceed their usual ranges; you should take similar care when improvising.

6.   As in our scale improvisations, while you practice make it a strict discipline to count aloud; you should know the precise measure number you are playing at any particular point in your improvisation.

7.   In order to familiarize your ear with the unique (if not exotic) modes outside the diatonic major and minor keys, practice a familiar tune with its traditional

harmonization in all modes. For example, play the hymn-tune "America" first in the key of C, carefully transposing its tune and harmony exactly. Then play the same hymn-tune in D, but without any accidentals, to feel a sense of the Dorian mode; in E for the Phrygian, and so on, taking care to keep the chords the same each time but never adding an accidental, playing only on the white keys. You will hear some very unusual voice-leading, to be sure, but you will come across some marvelous modal sonorities as well. We should be ever ambitious to open our ears to "new" sounds.

8. In order to practice phrases in different keys, you would do well to practice questions and answers concurrently with your scale improvisations, following the practice scheme suggested in Chapter 1. Both scale and phrase improvisations have so much in common that the benefits of practicing one greatly enhance practicing the other.

9. Develop and refine your phrase improvisations so that you achieve greater range in improvising brief interludes as part of your service-playing technique.

3. The Interlude

The improviser is frequently faced with the need to create smooth transitions from one portion of a liturgy or service to the next, to move unobtrusively from one piece of music to another, or from one event to the next. Certain actions need to be "covered" that have no predetermined length. Consider how unpredictable in terms of time these actions may be: collecting and presenting the offering, providing music for meditating, accommodating processions, or (horror of horrors) permitting the seating of latecomers by being expected to roll out a musical "red carpet" to welcome the errant worshiper! Flexibility in compressing or extending this improvised music is essential in making a complete musical statement that will in fact create a short composition, pleasing to the ear because of its well-structured form. Let us never consider "vamping" or "filling" or "ad libbing," terms anathema to the skilled musician!

In the previous chapter we developed, by improvising phrases, potential ways and means with which such transitions, or interludes, may be improvised. As a means of organizing interludes, we shall employ the basic unit of the phrase, using it as a building block. We shall think of phrases as modular units with which to assemble a larger musical structure. We will always be careful to design and control the space which these integral sections occupy so that clarity of form is always foremost.

1. Create an interlude that is an independent musical statement of known length, which may or may not include a change of keys. For example, a simple eight-measure question and answer may be improvised, based upon a melodic idea or a fragment suggested by a work that appears in the service; this phrase may be joined to a similar question and answer in, say, the dominant key; these two phrases may either stand as a double unit, or be expanded by a more elaborate or varied repetition of the first phrase back in the tonic key. Here we have either an eight- or sixteen- or twenty-four-measure piece.

Experiment by improvising such a piece, using Example 22 (Chap. 2), followed by Example 14 (Chap. 2) (changing the tempo to Lento, if you wish), and returning to Example 22 with some variation. Years of experience have taught me that there are two extremely useful and helpful means of organizing an improvisation: a "non-musical" or "written" outline—that is, an outline in words—and an outline in musical notation. The written outline would look like this:

Phrase 1: four-measure question plus four-measure answer (three voices, tonic key)
Phrase 2: four-measure question plus four-measure answer (two voices, dominant key)
Phrase 3: four-measure question plus four measure answer (three voices, tonic key, optional variations of phrase 1).

The repeating of phrase 1 might be made more interesting with even a slight amount of variation.

Example 1   (Chap. 2, Ex. 22 with some variation)

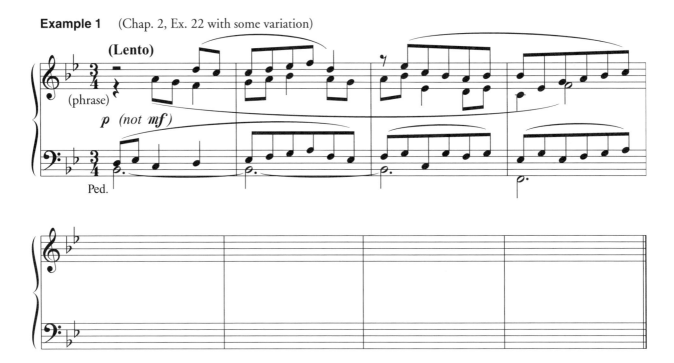

Note how easily variation is achieved by adding a fourth voice by means of a pedal point, and by adding a few passing or neighboring notes. Assembling such series of phrases in order to improvise such pieces will be fully explored in chapter 7.

2. Create an interlude that is an independent statement of predetermined length. Its purpose will be twofold: (1) to provide a transition from one portion of the liturgy to another, and (2) to modulate from the key of one piece to that of the next. The challenge is to maintain one style during the course of this transitional interlude.

The improviser will want to be able to move from key to key and style to style with ease and confidence. She or he will want to transform this practical necessity into an artistic entity, with every note carefully planned.

The most convincing modulating interludes are those built upon the phrase, which in turn is based upon thematic material already at hand. But before we proceed further, let us explore a basic technique of modulating.

Many musicians seem intimidated by the challenge of changing keys. In fact, planning a modulation is stimulating, much like solving a simple crossword puzzle. All keys are, in the end, related: given the keys of origin and destination, the improviser simply plots and plans the harmonic path to pursue by understanding the relationship between those two keys, however far apart they may appear. As we observed in Chapter 1, a solid foundation in harmony is vitally important.

The simplest and most basic approach is the identification of the dominant of a given key, then that dominant key's dominant, working one's way around that celebrated circle of fifths if necessary. We sometimes forget that parallel major and minor keys share the same dominant chord or key, and that those dominant keys need not always be major. For example, both C major and C minor share the same dominant chord or key of G—technically G major, but G minor is also possible. These realizations open up many helpful possibilities.

Consider that the key of C major moves naturally to G major; from here one may move to D major, B minor, F♯ minor, or several other keys whose signatures consist of sharps. Or, one might choose to move, by way of the dominant, to keys whose signatures contain flats, such as C major to G minor, D minor, B♭ major, F major or several other keys. A simple chart might help us to visualize these key relationships:

```
        F♯ minor                          F major
           ↑                                 ↑
D major ← G major ← C major → G minor → D minor
           ↓                                 ↓
        B minor                           B♭ major
```

Realizing these many options available, the improviser is in a position to chart her or his course, moving with ease and efficiency between even distantly related keys.

Here is an example of a modulation plan from A♭ minor to G major, two keys that, on the surface, seem not closely related:

Segment 1:   A♭ minor to E♭ major.

Segment 2:   E♭ major to C minor.

Segment 3:   C minor to G minor.

Segment 4:   G minor to D major.

Segment 5:   D major to G major.

This plan may be given its spatial structure by planning the number of measures for each phrase or segment. We will use our old friend, the four-measure phrase, for this illustration; of course, phrases or segments of any length may be used, so long as each chosen space is carefully planned. After choosing the time signature (it, too, may vary from segment to segment), our written outline would look like this:

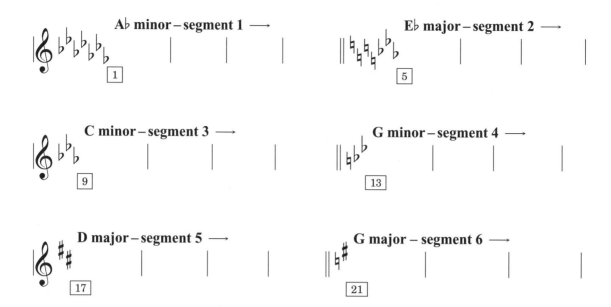

This is one of several possible plans; it is leisurely, rather like a "scenic route," for the modulation moves logically to one key, visiting it for awhile, and then moves on to the next key. As we shall see, each key may be revisited by moving backward by segments, thus lengthening the interlude to suit the time required for whatever action is taking place.

Using the phrase of Example 13 (Chap. 2), the interlude would look like this in musical notation:

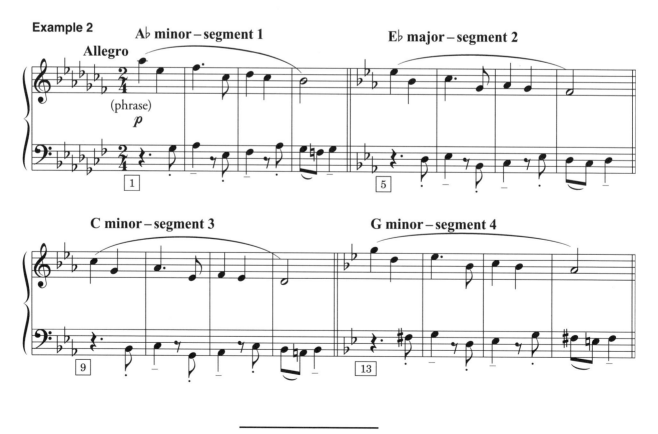

Example 2 (cont.)

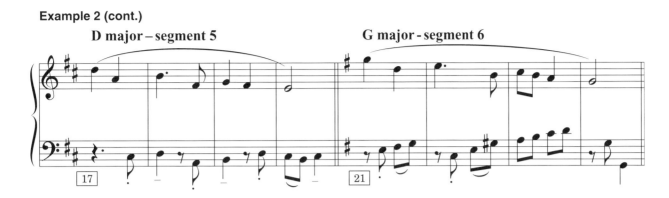

Note that each four-measure segment is a simple transposition of its original, with small alterations suggested by each key visited. Interest through variety might be achieved by embellishing or varying, however slightly, either the soprano or the bass.

Example 3

The improviser will want to conclude each segment in the style in which it began.

Note that, since we feel at home in any key, we will be able to play the segment on every note of the scale, diatonic and chromatic alike. A thorough practicing of the theme on each of those tones will not only give us assurance, but will also enable us to plan and improvise interludes with different and less conventional modulation plans. Play through the following phrase, then practice one half step up, continuing the pattern on all remaining tones of the chromatic scale:

Example 4

One might benefit by practicing these transpositions, with or without variations, before planning and then practicing the modulating interlude shown above.

In our interlude, we have the built-in option of compressing the length of the piece by moving from certain segments to others, making our "route" less "scenic," without jarring key changes. Here is such a possibility:

Segment 1 to   →   Segment 3 to → Segment 5 to →   G major

Conversely, we have the option of extending the length of the piece by reverting to the previous segment and even continuing backwards to earlier segments, then moving forward again. Here is one of several possibilities:

Segment 1 to   → Segment 2 to → Segment 3 to →

Segment 4 to   → Segment 3 to → Segment 4 to →

Segment 5 to   → Segment 4 to → Segment 5 to →   G major

Thus we enjoy almost limitless flexibility because of the modular structure of the plan, yet the form itself, however basic, cannot help but emerge. With each repetition of a given segment, variety will suggest itself and enhance the music.

3. Create an interlude that accompanies or "covers" a specific function within a liturgy and that provides a transition from the musical style of one piece to that of the next. In order to effect a convincing musical statement, we will begin our interlude by employing material from a piece previously performed and end by referring to the piece to follow. We shall again use our modular structure; segments will be based on thematic fragments from the selections immediately preceding and to come.

Let us assume that the choir has just performed "How lovely is thy dwelling place," from Brahms's *German Requiem,* as the offertory anthem:

There follows a logical need to connect the completion of the collection and the ushers' bringing of the alms to the altar, at which point the hymn "Praise God from Whom All Blessings Flow" will be sung by the congregation and choir to the tune "Old Hundredth":

This means that we shall move from the key of E♭ major in ¾ time to the key of G major in ⁴⁄₄ time. Within these guidelines we will determine the plan for moving from key to key in written outline form:

Segment 1:   E♭ major to C minor (four measures).

Segment 2:   C minor to G minor (four measures).

Segment 3:   G minor to D major (four measures).

Segment 4:   D major to G major (four measures).

We will next determine the distribution of the thematic materials from each of the two pieces, emphasizing the interlude's role as a musical transition. Here is a written plan:

Segment 1:   Measures 5 through 8 of the first theme of "How lovely is thy dwelling place," altering the segment's fourth measure in order to accommodate the key change, using the ¾ time signature.

Segment 2:   The same material as segment 1.

Segment 3:   The final phrase of "Old Hundredth," adapting the tune to suit our ¾ time signature.

Segment 4:   The final phrase of "Old Hundredth," adapting the tune to suit our ¾ time signature and changing that time signature to ⁴⁄₄ midway through this segment.

Here is how the thematic organization of the four segments will look in musical outline:

Example 5

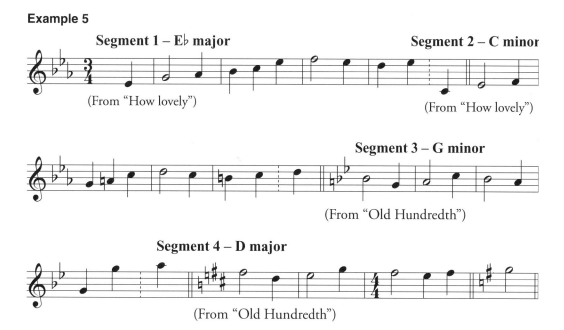

Segment 1 – E♭ major   **Segment 2 – C minor**

(From "How lovely")   (From "How lovely")

Segment 3 – G minor

(From "Old Hundredth")

Segment 4 – D major

(From "Old Hundredth")

Our next step will entail "dressing up" the interlude with harmonic and stylistic color. We may find it convenient to practice each segment by harmonizing the thematic materials with chordal progressions similar to those found in the chorus parts of the anthem, and continuing this harmonic style through the entire interlude.

Example 6 illustrates such a possibility. Note the optional left-hand part that employs elements from the anthem's accompaniment; although more complex, it enhances and more closely identifies the interlude as a musical transition:

Example 6

Right hand
(manual 1)

Left hand
(manual 1)

Optional L.H.
(manual 1)

Pedal

Example 6 (cont.)

Segment 3

Segment 4

Note again that we have the option of extending the length of the piece by reverting to previous segments. Here is one of several possibilities, beginning each segment with the up-beat after the dotted bar line:

Segment 1 to	→	Segment 2 to	→	Segment 3 to	→
Segment 4 to	→	Segment 3 to	→	Segment 1 to	→
Segment 3 to	→	Segment 4			

After practicing the segments several times, variations on each segment will naturally suggest themselves, giving more contrast and color as the interlude takes shape.

4. Create an interlude that modulates up a half-step. The improviser would benefit by being able to modulate, within a predetermined length of time, to the key one half step higher than the tonic of a piece. This customary technique stems from the occasional desire to have the final stanza of a hymn sung in the higher, brighter key in order to highlight the text and bring the hymn to a fuller climax. One accomplishes this most easily by simply thinking of the original tonic note as the leading tone of the key one half step higher. For example, G becomes the leading tone of A♭, A♭ of A (A♭ being the enharmonic equivalent of G♯), A of B♭, and so on.

The quickest and easiest way to accomplish this is simply to play those two chords in succession. (This is also a bit crude!) Let us assume that we want to move from the penultimate stanza, in the tonic key of G major, up to the key of A♭ major for a climactic final stanza. Here is such a modulation which, however abrupt, works:

Example 7

(From "Old Hundredth")

We might prefer a more subtle version of this modulation which will prepare the congregation for the new key, give everyone some breathing space, and add a moment of anticipation of what is to come:

Example 8

(From "Old Hundredth")

We shall fully explore the reharmonization of the final stanza, now up one half step, in Chapter 4.

Note that, by carefully using ascending and descending diatonic whole and chromatic half step motion within the various voices to manipulate the modulation, the starkly simple idea of the tonic note as the leading tone of the new key is more satisfyingly and convincingly accomplished, if not disguised.

Recommendations

1. Practice the theme of each phrase/segment in all keys and all modes so that you will be well prepared to plan the interlude. Choose thematic material with which you are comfortable and that appeals to you.

2. Design your plan very carefully and be firm with yourself about the number of measures that will comprise each segment, the number of segments you will need, and the logical ways in which these segments may be repeated and varied so that they make sense in terms of key and motivic relationship. Make a plan in written outline first; then write out as much of the plan in music notation as will be most helpful.

3. Practice each individual segment until it is completely mastered. Then move on to the next segment and master it with the same thoroughness.

4. After having practiced and refined the segments, practice them in different juxtapositions and configurations so that you will be able to improvise interludes of various predetermined lengths. Above all, aim and settle for only the interlude that gives you the most satisfaction and makes the most convincing musical statement.

4. The Hymn

The hallmark of a hymn is its repetitive nature. Most hymn tunes are played through once, then repeated several or even many times. In all art, repetition cries out for variety, and so, when leading the hymn singing, the improviser will want to enhance the meaning of the text by varying the manner in which the tune is played: changes in registration and harmony provide means by which any hymn tune may be given character and color.

We will follow several steps in learning to vary a hymn tune, few of which will retain the standard harmonizations of the tunes. Other steps will gradually depart from those harmonizations and lead to completely new settings of a given tune. Our liturgical purpose is to encourage the singing of a hymn by means of our musical goal, which is to extend and build our improvisational skills through restyling the tune's accompaniments. If the more elaborate improvisations are too complex to accompany some congregations, we might well use them instead for introducing the hymn in the service or to accompany a stanza sung only by the choir, practices for which there are ample historical precedents in the literature.

We will use a well known hymn tune, "Winchester New," harmonized by William Henry Monk:

Example 1

Before beginning to practice this hymn tune in various ways, practice the harmonization by playing the soprano part in the right hand on one manual (perhaps on a solo stop), the alto and tenor parts on another manual, and the bass part in the pedals. This will help free the hands from the dictates of the eyes, and prevent the musical vertigo that might otherwise result in steps 1 and 2 below by playing the notes in a position (and by a hand) different than is notated or customary. Further, such "soloing out" of a hymn tune is very useful in helping the congregation to grasp it, especially if it is new to them. Don't be discouraged if at first you find this difficult; write out an example on staff paper once or twice and then you will find that playing these examples becomes easier with each attempt.

1. Invert the alto and soprano parts, which creates a descant while leaving the harmony unchanged. Consecutive fifths appear in the soprano and the alto voices between beat 4 of measure 1 and beat 1 of measure 2; if you are bothered by this break of the rule in part-writing (and many of us may not be), simply leave out the offending passing tone D and replace it with the G above:

Example 2

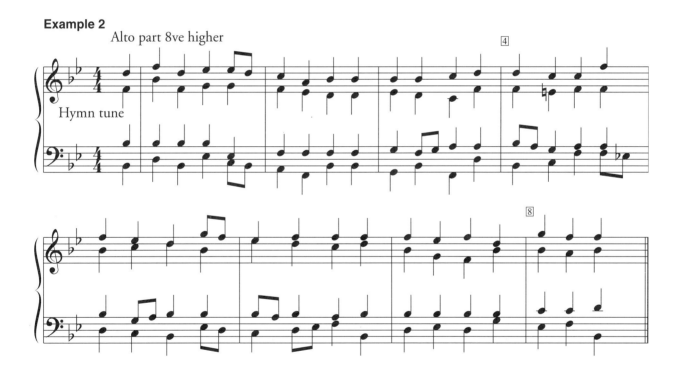

2. Invert the tenor and soprano parts. Again, a descant will emerge while the harmony remains unchanged. Again, consecutive fifths will appear, this time in the tenor voice (now moved up an octave from its original location), between beats 1 and 2 of measure 4; if you wish, either leave out the offending passing tone or replace it with the D just above it:

Example 3

Some musicians find that inverting by intervallic numbers (fourths to fifths, sixths to thirds, and so on) facilitates the process (this is certainly so in the case of octaves and unisons); others find that simple visual inversions (thinking up an octave) are easier. A combination of both methods is worth developing.

Note that in practicing step 2 at the organ, isolating the hymn tune in the left hand (now the new tenor voice) on another manual helps the player to focus more easily on the inversions taking place in each hand. This step also allows for the hymn tune (which is, after all, the focus) to be given prominence by means of registration; if, for example, it is played on a strong stop (such as a solo reed), it provides effective yet subtle leadership for the congregation through the contrast in timbre.

3. Add passing tones between notes which are separated by the interval of a third:

Example 4

More than one passing tone may be added between notes separated by wider intervals. For example, here are examples of such additions in the bass part:

Example 5

4. Add upper or lower neighboring tones between notes which are repeated:

Example 6

Note that we have shown neighboring tones between all repeated notes, regardless of the voice-leading or harmonic consequences. As a result, we have produced some very exotic and even bizarre sounds. Nevertheless, we should practice them all in order to gain facility. Then we will choose only those neighboring tones that make musical sense.

Now we will combine steps 3 and 4. Consecutive fifths or octaves may result, as in the upbeat to measure 1 and the first beat of measure 1: if you add a passing tone to the bass part and an upper neighboring note to the tenor part, consecutive octaves will occur; if, in order to avoid this situation, you add a lower neighbor to the tenor part, having added a passing tone to the alto part, imperfect but consecutive fifths will occur. In such cases, you will want to choose but one additional note, either passing or neighboring, and simply omit the other.

Example 7

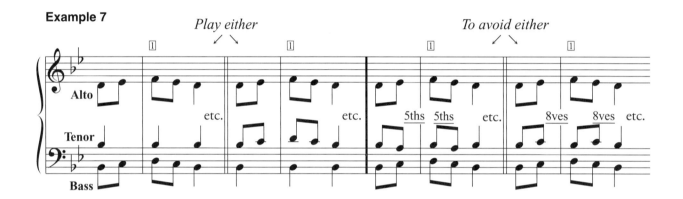

When an entire chord is repeated, as in measure 2, beats 3 and 4, choices should be made as to just which neighboring tone(s) will be played. Otherwise, decidedly unorthodox sonorities may jar the unsuspecting listener's ear:

Example 8

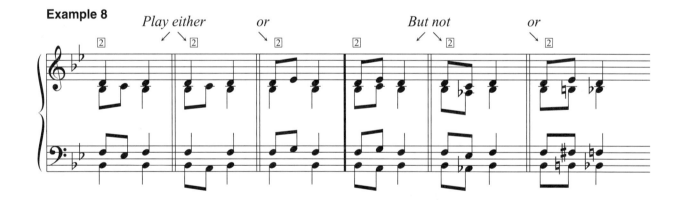

In the end, your ear and taste are your guides. If you are not offended by breaking the rules, simply play your version with conviction.

Here is an example of the combining of steps 3 and 4:

Example 9

We are now able to combine steps 1, 3, and 4; again, we have chosen only those extra notes we think work most suitably:

Example 10

We may now combine steps 2, 3, and 4:

Example 11

Technically speaking, we have begun to alter the original harmonization, although the chords on all four beats for each measure remain intact. We will now begin to change these chords' structure by means of suspensions.

5. *Create suspensions by delaying the downward movement of a voice part to which has been added a passing tone or an upper or lower neighboring note (indicated by the sign +).* Appoggiaturas may be created in a like manner: delay the upward arrival of a voice part to which has been added a passing tone or an upper or a lower neighboring tone (indicated by the sign ○).

Example 12

Note that we have created suspensions at almost every available opportunity; however, your sense of balance and taste will determine where and when suspensions should be played. In any event, suspensions add color and rhythmic interest. You are now able to improvise, using the combinations of steps 1 and 5, then 2 and 5. Write out versions of each of these combinations so as to facilitate improvising them at the keyboard.

6. Create a pedal-point by adding a fifth voice. No other single instrument is so capable of long and sustained pedal-points as the organ. We will begin by playing the pedal-point on the pedalboard (although, of course, a pedal-point may be created in any of the other voices, merely by reassigning and rearranging the existing four voices), playing the present soprano, alto, tenor, and bass voices on the manuals.

Here is the first phrase of our hymn tune in which we add a tonic pedal-point note (Bb) to a combination of steps 3 and 4:

Example 13

Here is the second phrase of our hymn tune in which we add the tonic pedal-point to a combination of steps 1, 3, and 4, changing to the supertonic (C) in measures 3 and 4:

Example 14

Here is the third phrase of our hymn tune in which we add the dominant pedal-point (F) to a combination of steps 2, 3, and 4:

Example 15

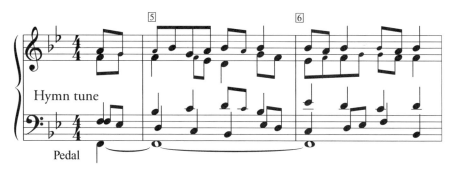

Here is the final phrase of our hymn tune, adding the dominant pedal-point (until the last beat of measure 8, when the tonic returns) to a combination of elements of steps 3, 4, and 5:

Example 16

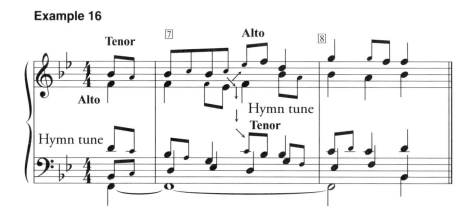

Within these four phrase fragments of our hymn tune, we have displayed a few possible combinations of steps. You will want to practice and master improvising in these combinations:

Steps 1 and 6
Steps 2 and 6
Steps 3 and 6
Steps 4 and 6
Steps 1, 3, and 6
Steps 1, 4, and 6
Steps 2, 3, and 6
Steps 2, 4, and 6
Steps 1, 3, 4, and 6
Steps 2, 3, 4, and 6
Steps 1, 3, 4, 5, and 6
Steps 2, 3, 4, 5, and 6

Experiment with different notes of the tonic scale as pedal-points, sustaining a given tone as long as possible, dissonances notwithstanding. Only when the dissonances become painfully discordant and the pedal-point hopelessly unworkable (usually during a modulation) should a change be made in the pedal-point. We thus continue to open our ears to new tonal possibilities.

7. *Create a descant by adding a fifth voice.* As we have seen, splendid descants can be created by manipulating both alto and tenor voices an octave higher. If we mix notes from these two voices and place them above the hymn tune, we can arrange a descant suitable for voices, organ, or other instruments to sing or play during the course of a stanza. Here is one of many possibilities:

Example 17

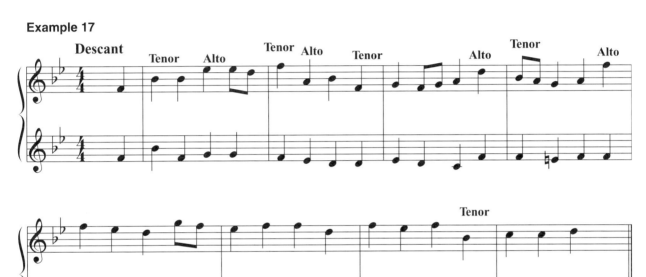

We will now want to compose a descant which is more independent rhythmically than the example above. We will choose three or four notes from the hymn tune, identify the scale degrees, and, through trial and error, find the best places for them to go. If we begin with the first four notes of the tune, F–B♭–F–G, the scale degrees are 5–8(1)–5–6. We will want to play this pattern on every scale degree of B♭ major, so that we can decide where best it will fit and enhance the tune.

Here is a possible solution:

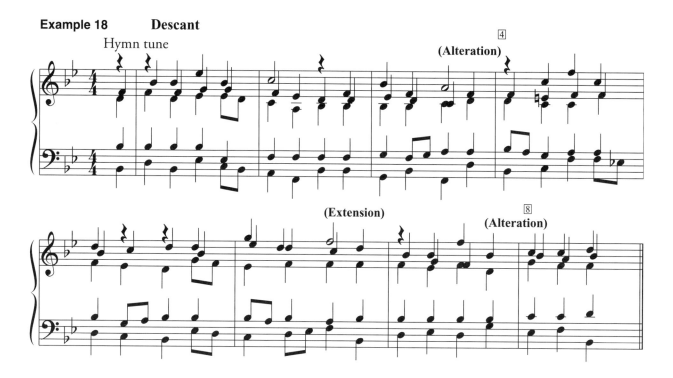

Example 18   Descant

Note that the independence of this descant enables it to answer the tune itself at regular distances. Also, in measure 3 and in measure 6 to the end, alterations of our melodic formula were needed in order to avoid undue dissonance. All kinds of such descants are possible, especially in conjunction with the other steps outlined above. Some of the most effective are those that appear briefly and even infrequently during the course of the hymn tune. One should not necessarily think of a descant as occupying every beat of a stanza.

8. *Create alternate chords for reharmonizing the hymn tune.* By this time, we have often departed from the original harmonization, and we will now deliberately seek to replace the given chords with others to create color and interest.

We will begin by playing the original harmonization in the opposite mode (B♭ minor, in this case), though the tune itself remains in its original major mode, for many musicians believe that the test of a first-rate hymn tune is its ability to sound well in either the major or the minor mode. Striking vertical sonorities will result by means of retaining the mode of the tune while simultaneously harmonizing it in its opposite mode.

Example 19

Virtually all the resulting alternate chords (indicated by the sign +) might be used, although a more judicious choice of only a few (indicated by the sign ⊞) would create greater effect. You will want to practice several versions, experimenting with various newly found chords replacing their originals.

Note that alternate chords themselves may be altered. For example, the bass note of beat 1, measure 4, might be changed from B♭ to B♮; the bass note of beat 1, measure 8, might be changed from E♭ to E♮; in that same chord, the tenor C♮ might be made a C♯, and, at the same time, the alto G♭ a G♮. All sorts of possibilities await. A simpler approach would be to practice the hymn tune throughout with the seventh scale degree lowered, excepting the tune itself, which, in all instances, we will keep intact.

Here is our hymn tune, reharmonized along such lines, with a few added passing and neighboring tones (and a little tenor flourish tossed in at the end):

Example 20

9. *Create an original harmonization of the hymn tune by improvising a new bass part or line.* This may be practiced in much the same fashion as we rehearsed harmonizations and accompaniments for our phrases earlier, limiting ourselves to a bass line which proceeds by step. The direction of the line may reverse itself, but initially we will avoid skips in order to discipline ourselves to a specific pattern. Here is the first phrase of the hymn tune, with a bass line that provides one note for each note of the tune (we will call this 1-on-1):

Example 21

the second phrase, with a bass line that has two notes for each note in the tune, or 2-on-1:

Example 22

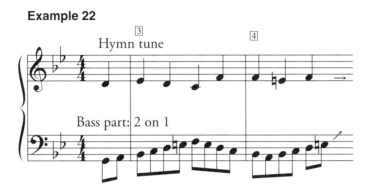

the third phrase, with a bass line that has three notes for each note of the tune, or 3-on-1:

Example 23

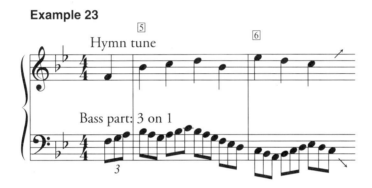

and the fourth phrase, with a bass line that has four notes for each note of the tune, or 4-on-1:

Example 24

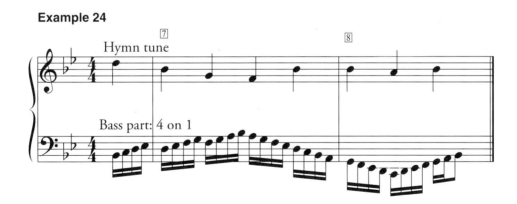

If these patterns are played in the pedals (with correct pedaling, of course), enhanced technique will be an additional dividend. The more we expand our musical "equipment," the better we will be able to improvise in all forms.

Note that, with a constantly moving bass line, unwanted dissonances are easily avoided by what amounts to long series of built-in passing tones. In other words, the new bass line may begin on almost any note and be made to work consonantly. If we vary the 1-, 2-, 3- or 4-on-1 patterns (equivalent to the various species in counterpoint) we have almost endless possibilities:

Example 25

These two voices can be made to work so well together that, with some refining, we might be able to construct a very brief hymn prelude from this idea (see Chapter 6).

When filling in the voices between a new bass part and the tune, we remember how well consecutive thirds and sixths work. To be sure, we will be confronted by some strange sonorities and inappropriate spacing between voices. Nevertheless, we might at least start with these consonant intervals, making adjustments later on, after we have practiced them several times in differing configurations. Here is the first phrase of our hymn tune, with both the tune and the newly improvised bass line attended by consecutive thirds:

Example 26

the second phrase with both the tune and the bass harmonized in sixths:

Example 27

the third phrase, with the tune attended by thirds and the bass by sixths:

Example 28

and the fourth phrase, with the tune in sixths and the bass in thirds:

Example 29

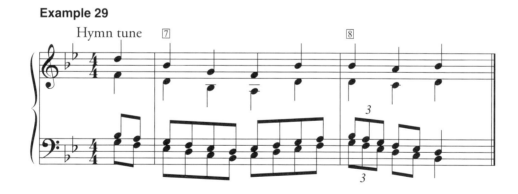

These examples illustrate only the initial stages; we are not suggesting such harmonies for public consumption. But from such practicing will emerge other ideas; adjustments in chords and voice-leading will be suggested; eventually, with the use of altered chords and other techniques we have now acquired, a new and fresh harmonization will evolve, leading us to further refinement and experimentation.

10. Create passages to supply rhythmic and harmonic interest where long notes appear in the hymn. Most hymn tunes have long notes at the ends of certain phrases, at the halfway point, and at the end. In some versions of "Winchester New," the third beats in measures 4 and 8 appear as dotted half notes. We may supply these rhythmic vacuums with passing tones, upper and lower neighboring notes, and suspensions improvised during those three beats.

Here is but one example of how we might thus treat measure 4:

Example 30

and measure 8:

Example 31

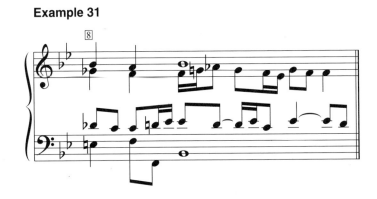

Note that in measure 4, no extra beats are added, whereas measure 8, since it is the close of the hymn tune, is extended by an extra quarter beat.

11. Create a hymn improvisation, combining, in as confluent a fashion as possible, steps 1 through 10. What follows below is an example of what may be improvised upon our modest and unsuspecting "Winchester New," distributing the hymn tune in different voices as indicated:

Example 32

Recommendations

1. Practice each step until fully mastered, beginning with a written version and proceeding to the keyboard. This is essential.

2. As you master each step thoroughly, begin to combine them; but master each combination before moving to the next (see step 6 for combination suggestions). Of course, not all steps will fit well together; much depends on the original harmonic properties of each hymn tune. Do not be discouraged, and do not hesitate to experiment, however unusual to your ear the result might be. Note, however, that any and all of these steps are applicable to any hymn tune, regardless of its harmonic properties.

3. Remember that the hymn tune itself is the focal point and must be treated with much care.

4. Remember the congregation at all times. It should be alerted as to which stanza will be reharmonized, either in the service bulletin or by the way you customarily begin the improvised stanzas (perhaps by playing the first few notes—or even the entire first phrase, if it is short—in octaves). We improvise on hymns, adding variation, color, and vitality, precisely to inspire congregational singing. If instead we confuse the congregation and impede their singing, we have defeated our purpose.

5. Suggested approaches to harmonizing the hymn tune in step 9 may be applied to virtually any form of music, as we will later see.

6. In writing out sketches of some of these steps (especially 3 and 4), a dot on the appropriate line or space of your hymnal might suffice to indicate just where your alterations will or will not be occurring. This method will make the eye more alert to possibilities and prepare you for writing out the more elaborate and complex improvisations with greater efficiency. This, in turn, will greatly facilitate your improvising at the keyboard.

5. The Ornamented Hymn

The sturdy and noble hymn tune provides the foundation for improvisations simple or complex. Such improvisations may be used as a means of introducing a hymn to the congregation within the context of a service. Or they may exist as independent pieces serving as preludes, interludes, postludes, and meditative reflections of hymns just sung.

We will begin the practice of such improvisations by placing the hymn tune in one voice with only one other voice to accompany it. We will think of this construction as an adaptation of the sixteenth-century *bicinium* (two-part) form. Next we will add a third voice to this plan, improvising in the traditional *tricinium* (three-part) form. The striking feature of the *bicinium* and the *tricinium* forms is that the hymn tune, or cantus firmus, appears note-by-note from its beginning to its end, without interruption of any kind (save phrasing, of course). This characteristic sets it apart from hymn preludes, which we shall explore at length in the following chapter.

Our aim at the beginning is for simplicity. Gradually, we will arrive at a point whereby some elaboration, by means of ornamentation, will begin to suggest itself. The texture is transparent; the hymn tune is the primary voice and the improvising takes place in the other voice or voices.

So that we will not be influenced by hymnals' harmonizations, we will work with only the tune.

1. Create an ornamented hymn in two voices on the tune "St. Anne," with the hymn tune in the treble clef and the accompanying voice in the bass clef. We will not concern ourselves with counterpoint in the strict sense, but rather with improvising sounds that please us. First we will practice one note in the left hand for each note in the right:

Example 1

The added voice need not be thought of as a bass part.

Next we place the tune in the left hand and the accompanying voice, still note against note, in the right:

Example 2

Accompanying voice

Hymn tune

Again, the added voice need not necessarily be thought of as the soprano part or melody.

Reverting to our first version, we then begin to add notes to the accompanying voice in the left hand. These added notes may be passing tones or upper or lower neighboring tones. We are wise to avoid skips at this stage; after we have mastered the scale-like treatment of the accompanying voice, wider intervals will suggest themselves, whereas essaying random leaps at the outset might, without sufficient control, cause unwanted and inhibiting sonorities.

Example 3

Hymn tune

Accompanying voice

Next we reverse the procedure as before by placing the hymn tune in the left hand and the improvised accompanying material in the right:

Example 4

Accompanying voice

Hymn tune

We will now expand the accompanying voice by giving it a rhythmic identity. One of the most familiar patterns in keyboard literature is the eighth note followed by two sixteenth notes: ♪♬ ♪♬. This pattern will give us more space, flexibility, and character, even if we adhere to our basically scale-wise plan for the accompanying voice.

Example 5

Hymn tune

Accompanying voice

Another well-known rhythmic pattern in keyboard literature is the grouping of
triplets for each beat: :

Example 6

Accompanying voice

Hymn tune

Note that, at this point, the hymn tune is beginning to want some decoration to
balance the activity in the accompanying voice.

_2. Create an ornamented hymn in two voices with the hymn tune appearing in first
one voice and then the other._ Here is an opportunity to add interest and variety by the
alternation of voices and ranges for the cantus firmus. We shall also try to give the
hymn tune more character by adding some decorations to it, such as passing tones,
upper and lower neighboring notes, and primary ornaments such as the mordent,
which traditionally starts on the principal note:

or the short trill of three or four notes, which usually, by tradition, starts on the note
above the principal note:

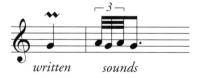

Our goal is to start simply as we practice these examples for improvising.

Example 7

Because the piece is built on the hymn tune, we have a solid and constant foundation that will give us greater support and confidence, both as we begin and as we extend and elaborate our improvisations. Remember that the accompanying voice may be stripped of as many notes as desired; that is, it may be as uncomplicated as we wish, especially in the beginning stages of our practicing.

3. Create an ornamented hymn in three voices, with the decorated hymn tune appearing in the top voice. The bottom voice will now, of necessity, become a bass part, and the middle voice will supply the harmony implied by the bass part as support for the cantus firmus. We shall begin building the elaborated cantus firmus by using the decorations found in Example 7:

Example 8

We will want to be able to reverse the top and middle voices, placing the hymn tune in the middle voice, with the middle voice now becoming the top voice. In most cases, a simple inversion of those two parts will work very nicely. Slightly more ambitious is the placement of the decorated cantus firmus in the bottom voice. In this instance, one should not necessarily think of the hymn tune as a true bass part, but rather as the third voice in a three-part piece.

We should begin our practice by supplying the missing measures of the examples. We should emphasize simplicity at first, especially in the middle and bottom voices. This approach has the advantage of allowing the decorated and ornamented cantus firmus its due prominence. Possible passing tones, repeated notes, upper and lower neighboring notes, and other notes that create a triad, in whatever inversion, are suggested in small notes as options.

Note that we are not in the least obliged to work within any given style or any particular period of music. Here we have begun with an eighteenth-century dialect simply because so much of the keyboard literature from which we readily find examples comes to us from that golden epoch. In the beginning, we should not be inhibited by adhering strictly to "the rules."

Recommendations

1. The ornamented hymn lends itself equally well to both simple and elaborate embellishments. We should never lose confidence in attempting to improvise such music, for the hymn tune is the cantus firmus, fixed before us as a guide at all times, and thus dictates the true structure of the piece.

2. The improviser will want to devise her or his plan very carefully, mindful of the many techniques learned in the previous chapters. To practice the final plan, one needs only the hymn tune, without the influence of any previous harmonizations, as the sole material with which to work.

3. Once the basic plan is determined, the improviser will want to practice the music in precisely the same way keyboard players practice other literature: in *bicinia*, hands separately and together; in *tricinia*, right hand and pedals, left hand and pedals, manuals alone, and manuals with pedals. (Does this sound familiar?) Consequently, one learns to listen to each part, to take each voice with equal seriousness, and to focus on each resulting sonority.

4. Do not think of the ornamented hymn as a form confined to any one historical style; the voices need not be contrapuntal nor even consonant.

6. The Hymn Prelude

The hymn or chorale tune provides the improviser with far-ranging opportunities for creating music, and, as a cantus firmus, is in fact a staple in a vast amount of keyboard literature. The development of musical ideas springing from phrases or even fragments of a tune in a hymn or chorale prelude lends unity and structure in both design and thematic exploitation. The listener's interest is heightened by a familiarity with the tune and its motifs.

Many forms of such cantus firmus–based preludes have evolved during the past few centuries. We will choose but a few of the more well-known forms with which to begin. Again, we shall greatly over-simplify these forms for purposes of initial practicing.

We now possess an extraordinary array of techniques: fluency in all keys; control of space; ability to harmonize and to invent bass lines; and capacity for elaboration of melody and accompaniment, to mention but a few. In particular, we shall employ and expand the new techniques just learned in Chapter 5.

1. *Create an elaborated and embellished hymn or chorale tune, improvised with a simple accompaniment, called the ornamented hymn prelude.* The length of such a work will be determined by the length of the tune itself. Since we have become much attached to "Winchester New," we might just as well use it for our first improvisations.

Here is a verbal outline for our improvisation:

Phrase 1	Measures 1–2	4 voices
Interlude	Measure 3	3 voices
Phrase 2	Measures 4–5	4 voices
Interlude	Measure 6	3 voices
Phrase 3	Measures 7–8	4 voices
Interlude	Measure 9	3 voices
Phrase 4	Measures 10–11	4 voices
Interlude*	Measure 12	4 voices

*(extension of phrase 4)

Note that we have built in four intervening sections in which the tune is not heard, and in measure 12, the tune becomes a part of a coda or an epilogue-like interlude. Models for such a form can readily be found in the works of Buxtehude and Bach, among many others. It was a favorite and important form in German Baroque music.

Here is an outline for our improvisation:

Example 1

If improvised at the organ, the melody may be played as a solo, with the bass played in the pedals.

Note that the way in which we have improvised the embellished and ornamented tune is an outgrowth of the technique we began to develop in the ornamented scale improvisations (see Chap. 1, Ex. 38).

You may prefer, in this instance, to practice improvising from the musical outline first. Continue the voice lines begun above, thinking of each voice as possessing its own distinct and characteristic identity. Write out a completed version of Example 1, check it at the keyboard, practice improvising with it, and then switch to the written outline for practice. Select another tune and repeat the process. Remember that this form works just as well in two- and three-voice textures.

2. *Create a hymn prelude that emphasizes the tune by placing it in long note values.* Improvise voices above, below, or around it that move in parallel motion (here again, thirds and sixths will work very nicely) or contrary motion, and that will become independently contrapuntal in nature. We will christen this form the *organ hymn prelude.* Here is a written outline for our improvisation:

Phrase 1	Measures 1–5	2 or 3 voices
Interlude	Measures 5–6	1 or 2 voices
Phrase 2	Measures 6–10	2 or 3 voices
Interlude	Measures 10–11	1 or 2 voices
Phrase 3	Measures 11–15	2 or 3 voices
Interlude	Measures 15–16	1 or 2 voices
Phrase 4	Measures 16–20	2 or 3 voices
Interlude*	Measures 20–22	2 or 3 voices

*(extension of phrase 4)

Note that this outline is almost identical to that preceding it. Again, there are many models for this form readily found in the works of Pachelbel, Buxtehude, and, as always, Bach, among others.

Here is a musical outline for our improvisation in two voices:

Example 2

Note how we are able to use the techniques previously acquired in composing bass lines for phrases (see Chap. 2, Ex. 54). Here is a musical outline for our improvisation in three voices:

Example 3

Note how we emphasize the sequence in designing the other voice parts. This device not only shapes and unifies, it allows independence of each voice while simultaneously creating interdependence among them.

Of course, these examples are mere suggestions. For instance, an ornamented cantus firmus line, as in Example 1, would give greater interest and flavor to the piece. We must always seek to combine and recycle those elements, devices, and techniques already acquired.

3.   _Create a hymn prelude by improvising interludes between the main sections of the cantus firmus._ We will call this form _the interpolation prelude._ At last (sadly?) we leave our beloved "Winchester New." Here is the hymn tune "Hyfrydol," followed by the written outline of an improvisation based on that tune:

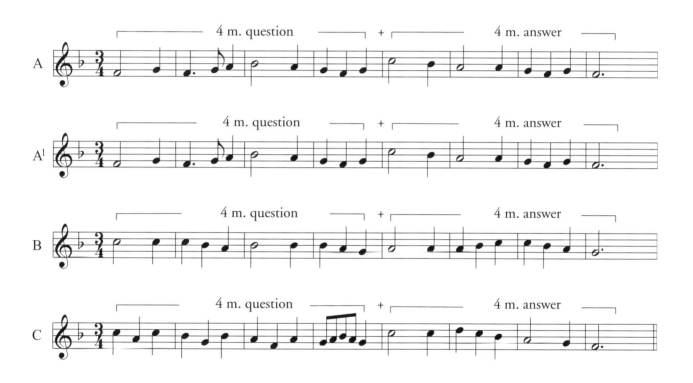

Section	Phrase	Number of voices	Interpolation	Number of voices	Measure numbers
A	4 m. q + 4 m. a	4	+ 4 m. a¹	3	1–12
A¹	4 m. q + 4 m. a	4	+ 4 m. a¹	3	13–24
B	4 m. q + 4 m. a	4	+ 4 m. a¹	3	25–36
C	4 m. q + 4 m. a	4	+ 4 m. a¹	3	37–48

Note that we are again working within the song form structure, since this particular hymn tune is so constructed. The tune of the A section is repeated; hence, the A¹ designation is used. The interpolations are but refashionings of the answers in each section;

they are set off and contrasted by a reduced number of voices, which lends textural variety as well, and are designated as answer[1] (a[1]). There are many models for this form readily found in the works of such composers as Brahms, Karg-Elert, and Sowerby.

We may also add an optional introduction and/or coda (epilogue):

Introduction:	4 mm.	3 or 4 voices	Measures i–iv
		and/or	
Coda (Epilogue):	4 mm.	3 or 4 voices	Measures 49–52

We will want to use thematic materials from the cantus firmus for these added sections, in order to anticipate the tune in the introduction, to reflect on the tune in the coda, and to give unity to the entire work.

The written outline may be practiced side-by-side with your hymnal opened to the tune "Hyfrydol." However, in order to develop skill and sophistication in mastering this and most other forms, we will begin by supplying the missing notes, lines, and empty measures in the musical outline:

Example 4

Note that thematic material from section (phrase) C is used in both the introduction and the coda (epilogue).

In section (phrase) A¹, the cantus firmus is moved to the tenor voice (as in step 2 of our hymn improvisation method), and A¹ is harmonized in the relative key of D minor (as in our scale and phrase improvisations) to provide contrast.

There is considerable use of parallel motion (as in the harmonizations of our phrase improvisations).

The tune is occasionally ornamented or elaborated (as in our ornamented hymn prelude improvisations). These references to earlier techniques illustrate the cumulative nature of improvisatory technique. Using skills already mastered will also inspire confidence; I encourage you to use them as frequently as possible as you advance.

This form is extremely flexible; many variations in design and configuration are possible—one could experiment, for example, with differing amounts of space.

As always, follow our usual practice routine: supply music for the empty measures, write out an example and check it at the keyboard, and practice from the written outline. Then plan, sketch, and practice improvising an interpolation prelude on a cantus firmus of your choice, repeating the same procedure.

4. Create a hymn prelude by improvising interludes or interpolations that precede rather than follow each phrase section of the cantus firmus. These interpolations will differ markedly: they will be contrapuntal and fugal in nature. Each voice will enter at a designated point and will be based on the cantus firmus phrase that is to follow each completed interpolation; the cantus firmus will appear in long note values (as in the earlier organ hymn prelude). We will call this form *the point-of-imitation hymn prelude.* We choose the hymn tune "St. Thomas," which consists of three four-measure phrases, each of which might be thought of as a two-measure question plus a two-measure answer:

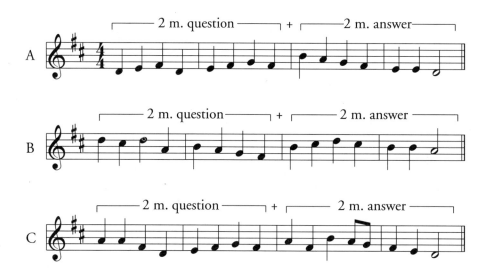

The entries for the points of imitation will appear in quarter-note values, and will be built on the two-measure questions themselves; the cantus firmus proper will appear in half-note values. The piece will be set for three voices, and thus there will be three entries, one for each voice. The top voice will become the cantus firmus, the bottom voice the bass, and the middle voice the remaining contrapuntal line.

Here is a written outline for our improvisation. Unlike the other outlines, it is horizontal rather than vertical:

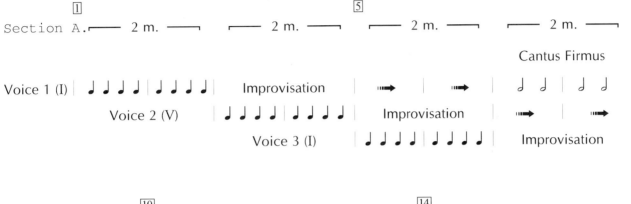

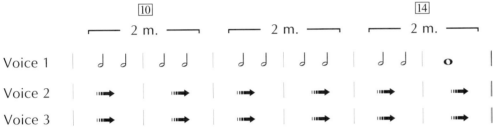

Section B. Measures 15 through 28 as in A.

Section C. Measures 29 through 42 as in A and B, with an optional coda/extension of perhaps 2 measures.

There are many models for this form readily found in the works of Pachelbel (for whom it has even been nicknamed!), Buxtehude, Brahms, Sowerby, and, most sublimely, Bach.

Here is the musical outline:

Example 5

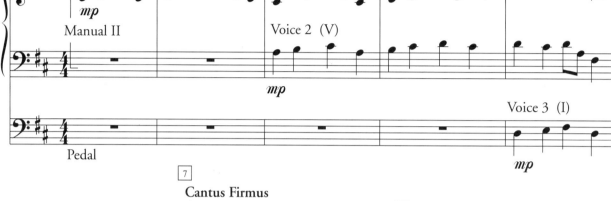

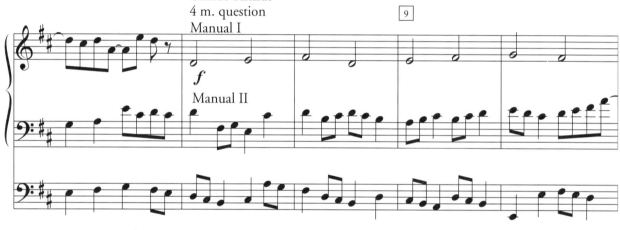

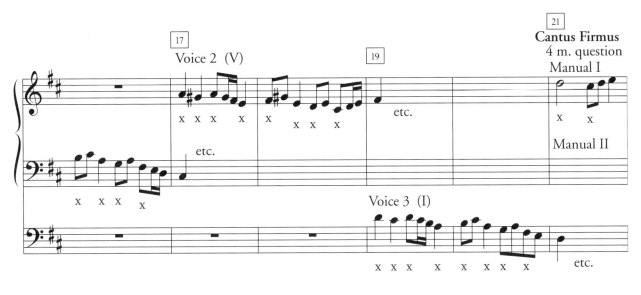

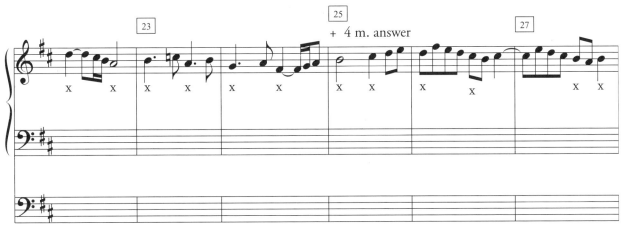

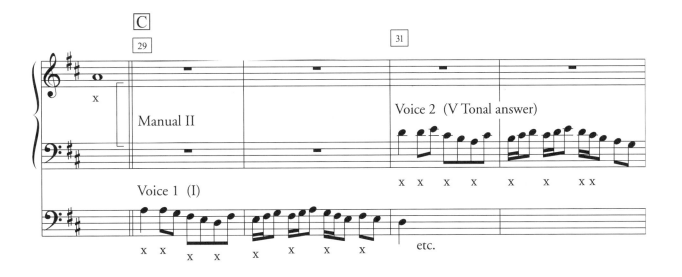

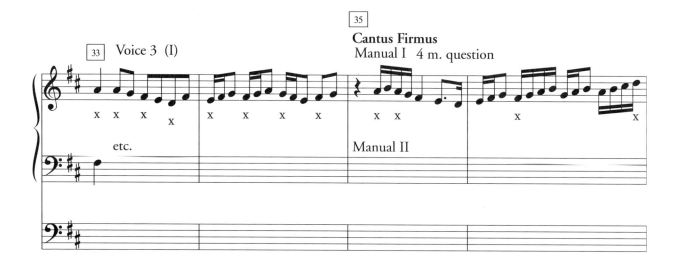

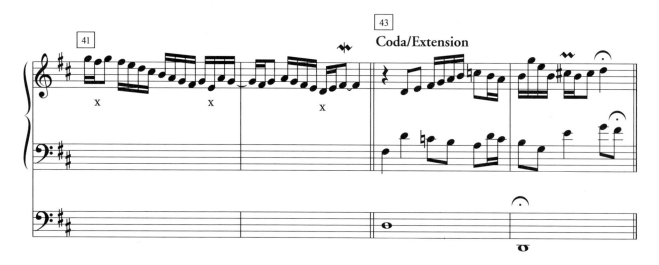

Note that in each section the order of entries varies (compare measures 1, 15, and 29), lending interest to the piece. Also, sections A, B, and C become more complex, demonstrating both simple and more elaborate treatments. One should select a certain level of complexity for one's improvisation and maintain consistency throughout. Your ability to elaborate on the points-of-imitation and ornament the cantus firmus will naturally evolve as you continue to practice and experiment. Remember that independence of voices, achieved through contrary motion and differing rhythms, is important in the contrapuntal style demanded by this form; therefore relatively few consecutive parallel intervals occur.

As with most organ literature, one will benefit greatly from practicing these improvisations in this age-old, never-failing sequence: hands together, right hand and pedal, left hand and pedal, all together. Also, it will be wise to practice this or any other form in sections: the points-of-imitation (measures 1–6, 15–20, and 29–34), then the remaining cantus firmus portions.

This form can be made to work for any hymn or chorale tune; special designs will suggest themselves in relation to the phrase lengths of the given tune. It may be adapted for two voices by simply eliminating the third voice and the last two measures of each of the point-of-imitation sections, and may even be improvised in four or five voices. The first section of the written outline would look like this:

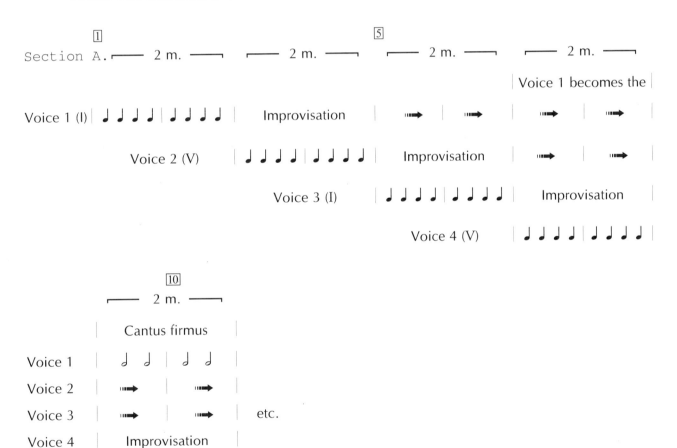

The piece would then proceed as before, remaining the same for sections B and C, with Voice 1, as before, metamorphosing into the cantus firmus.

Smoother transitions between the cantus firmus and point-of-imitation sections may easily be arranged by overlapping the retirement and re-entry of each voice, usually in the order of appearance. This obviates the complete textural and rhythmic halt at the end of each section. Here is a musical outline of such an instance, using measures 14–19:

Example 6

Note that Voice 1, the first to appear in measure 1, is the first to retire (measure 14) and the first to re-enter (measure 15); voices 2 and 3 follow suit in exactly the same pattern. To ensure continuity, the same voices begin in the same order for each point-of-imitation section; in our first version, we varied the order of the voices' entries. Regardless of the scheme chosen, both styles should be practiced.

5. *Create a hymn fantasy (fantasia).* The term "fantasy" is often misleading to musicians, who might interpret the concept as one of total abandon (always a dangerous attitude with which to approach an improvisation—or any attempt at creativity, for that matter). The form should be as meticulously planned (down to the last sixteenth rest) as all our other forms have been. We will begin to organize a fantasy by using elements and techniques already practiced and mastered. For example, we might put together sections utilizing elements of the hymn preludes for a fantasy on "St. Thomas." Here is a written outline:

Section	Form/Style	Number of voices	Number of measures	Measures
A	Interpolation Prelude:			
	Introduction	4	4	1–4
	Ornamented Prelude:			
	Phrase 1: 4 m. q	4	4	5–8
	Interpolation	3	2	9–10
	Ornamented Prelude:			
	Phrase 1: 4 m. a	4	4	11–14
B	Point-of-imitation Prelude:			
	Points-of-imitation	1–3 (or 4)	6	15–20
	Phrase 2: 4 m. q + 4 m. a	3 (or 4)	8	21–28
	Interpolation	3	2	29–30
C	Hymn Prelude:			
	Phrase 3: 4 m. q	3	4	31–34
	Interpolation /Sequence	4	4	35–38
			(2 2-m. units)	
	Interpolation Prelude:			
	Phrase 3: 4 m. a	4	4	39–42
	Interpolation/Points-of-			
	imitation: Coda/Epilogue	4 (or 5 or 6)	4 (or 8)	43–46
				(or 43–50)

Here is a musical outline:

Example 7 — Hymn Fantasy on "St. Thomas"

Throughout the outline, the cantus firmus always appears in augmented note values. Again, this scheme is arbitrary and is only one of a countless number of possibilities. Combining, connecting, interweaving, and juxtaposing styles, forms, and elements permit enormous ranges of choices.

Recommendations

1. Remember to count aloud while practicing, especially from the written outlines, in order to ensure total control of space for each section.

2. As we practice keyboard literature, so should we practice our improvising: by voice, phrase, and section, before putting everything together. Refining the final work follows inevitably.

3. Choose models of each form from the master composers; learn from careful analysis how to craft and develop your own personal musical style.

7. The Song Form

You are now prepared to improvise in larger, more extended structures. We will begin with song forms. Using as building blocks the eight-measure phrases we now improvise so well, we can outline sections A and B of our song form:

A Four-measure question plus four-measure answer in the tonic key.
B Four-measure question plus four-measure answer beginning in a key other than the tonic, but returning to end in the tonic.

The sections in this sixteen-measure piece of music should be so constructed as to contrast with each other rhythmically, thematically, and in contour; yet they should relate to each other in character, style, and mood.

Here is a musical outline of the same piece:

Example 1

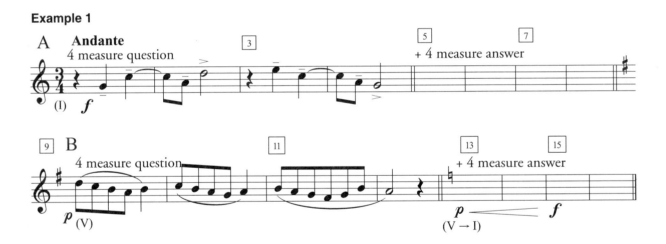

Note that section A is in the tonic key of C (indicated as I) and is characterized by its intervallic skips and sequential nature (making it easily recognizable by the listener with whom the performer should always seek to communicate). Section B is, as the added F# attests, in the dominant key of G (indicated by V), and is contrastingly characterized by its unrelenting stepwise, scale-like nature, also sequential; B, however, will return to the tonic in its answer, indicated by the natural sign. Here are two of countless possible answers, one to A and one to B, combining elements of both sections so as to bring the piece to a satisfying conclusion. The double bar lines used to set off each question, answer, and section are visual aids in defining space.

Example 2

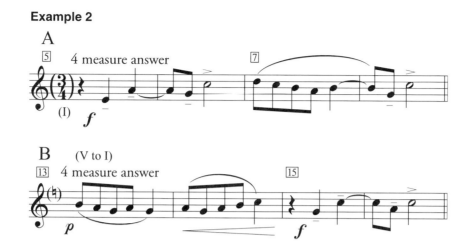

Remember that numbering our measures is merely a visual form of counting aloud as we practice with only the written outline before us. At this stage we are expert at counting aloud as we practice improvisation or literature; this enables us to analyze the music so that we understand what is taking place developmentally, and so that we become unable to lose our place or suffer a memory slip when performing.

We will now expand our treatment by extending the AB form to ABA[1]. Here we simply remain in the tonic for A, move to the dominant for B, and return to the tonic for A[1]. A[1] will differ from A through slight variations and ornamentation; this provides interest and richness. First, the written outline:

A (I)	4 m. question + 4 m. answer
B (V)	4 m. question + 4 m. answer
A[1] (I)	4 m. question + 4 m. answer

Here is a musical outline of the same piece:

Example 3

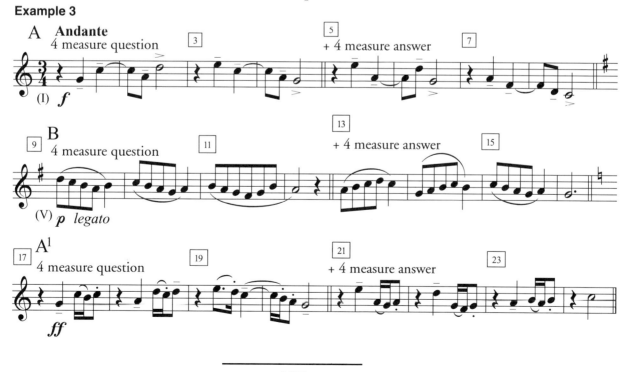

Note that the return of A is slightly varied and simply ornamented; this is an unnecessary but useful device and practice which adds interest and richness to the piece. We will be able therefore to call it A prime (A[1]).

No modulation is required in moving from I to V and back to I, since the keys are so closely related. Within the boundaries of traditional harmony, other related keys would be the subdominant (IV), the relative minor (VI) in a major key, and the relative major in a minor key (III).

We might well expand our form from ABA[1] to ABA[1]CA[1] or even ABA[1]CA[1]BA[1]. Examples 1 and 2 are sixteen measures long and Example 3 twenty-four measures. We can expand even further to forty- and fifty-six-measure pieces.

Here is a written outline for section C in the closely related and nicely contrasting relative minor key of A (VI):

      C (VI)   4 m. question + 4 m. answer

Here is the musical outline of the same section:

Example 4

The configuration of this section borrows freely from both sections A and B, using the wide intervals of A and the scalewise contour of B; by relating the themes to each other despite their contrasts, we create a unified work. We might expand even further, creating a rondo-like form: ABA[1]CA[1]DA[1]; ABA[1]CA[1]DA[1]B[1]A[1]; ABA[1]CA[1]B[1]A[1]DA[1]; ABA[1]CA[1]B[1]A[1]DA[1]C[1]A[1]B[1]A[1]; ABA[1]CA[1]B[1]DA[1]B[1]D[1]A[1]B[1]A[1]C[1]A[1]D[1]A[1]; and so on. The number of possibilities is immense because of our use of sections as building blocks within our unit-oriented construction process.

Here is a musical outline for section D in the closely related subdominant key of F:

Example 5

Since section C was virtually an amalgam of sections A and B, we have here created an anomalous section that is in sharp contrast to the other two.

At this point we will practice the expansion of any given unit of the piece. For example, A might be doubled in length, and thus become a double statement of the section's musical theme.

Here is the written outline:

A (I)   4 m. question + 4 m. answer

plus

4 m. question + 4 m. answer

We will want to reiterate the question in either measure 9 or 13 (or perhaps, in modified form, in both), in order to give coherence and balance to the section.

Here are musical outlines of an expanded A in which the question is repeated in measure 9:

Example 6

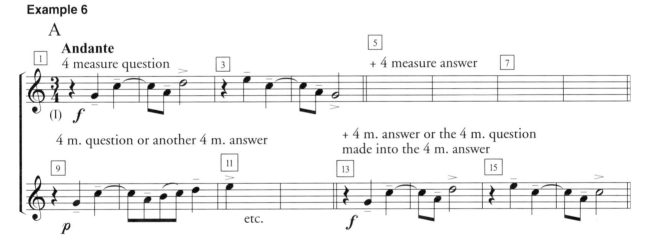

measure 13:

Example 7

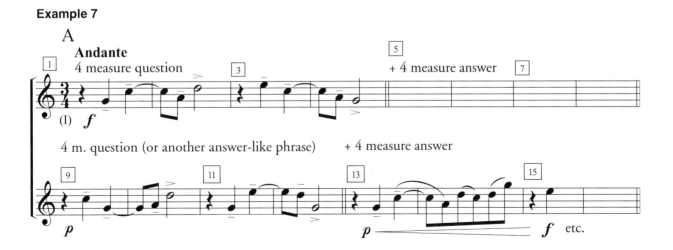

or, in modified forms, in both measures 9 and 13:

Example 8

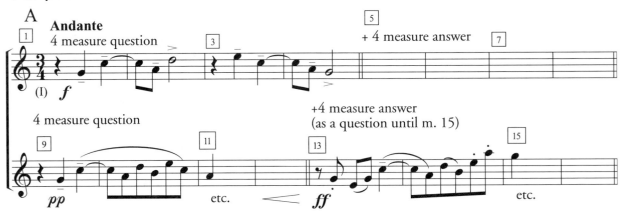

Note that the answer of measure 5 may move to a key other than I, so as to set up measure 9; by the same token, measure 9 might be reharmonized in another key (such as VI), so as to set up the final return in measure 13 of the tune. Conversely, measure 8 might end as convincingly in the tonic. Any kind of musical rhetoric, so long as it is truly interesting, only lends thematic unity to the improvisation.

Based upon the preceding ideas and elements, we are now prepared to design a piece of music. Given the myriad choices and opportunities at our disposal, we will choose a fairly extended form, employing the expanded section three times. Here is the written outline of the form (ABA^{1}CA^{1}DA^{1}B^{1}A^1) we will practice:

Section	Key	Number of voices	Question	Answer	Measures
A	I	4	4 mm.	4 mm.	1–8
	I	4	4 mm.	4 mm.	9–16
B	V	3(or 2)	4 mm.	4 mm.	17–24
A^1	I	4(or 3)	4 mm.	4 mm.	25–32
C	VI	3	4 mm.	4 mm.	33–40
	VI	3(or 2)	4 mm.	4 mm.	41–48
A^1	I	3(or 4)	4 mm.	4 mm.	49–56
D	IV	2(or 3) (or 4)	4 mm.	4 mm.	57–64
A^1	I	4(or 3) (or 2)	4 mm.	4 mm.	65–72
B^1	V	3(or 4)	4 mm.	4 mm.	73–80
	V	4(or 2) (or 3)	4 mm.	4 mm.	81–88
A^1	I	4	4 mm.	4 mm.	89–96

and the musical outline (note that we will begin to think in terms of more than one voice):

Example 9

Example 9 (cont.)

Example 9 (cont.)

The section themes appear only as questions, with several variations. You will want to practice this piece by supplying the answers and the other voices.

All markings for dynamic changes, phrasing, articulation, and other indications are missing, so that you are free to experiment as you practice.

We have been arbitrary in designing this piece. Many different designs are possible; the form is extremely flexible and can be varied in many ways. For example, A or A¹ need not necessarily appear between each of the other sections; you might choose to proceed directly from B to C, or from C to D.

It is not necessary or even desirable to end each answer in whatever the current key might be; the answer can become a natural and helpful transition to the next section. For example, the answer in B, beginning at measure 21, might very well modulate and lead back to the tonic, setting up the return of A¹:

Example 10

Or, in a like manner, the answer to one of the A¹ sections might lead in to the subsequent section, as in measure 53:

Example 11

The number of voices for each section is deliberately varied, thereby lending character and contrast.

There are many options for placing the section themes in different ranges and registers, even during the course of the section itself. For example, the question might be given in the soprano and answered in the tenor.

The song form is infinitely flexible; it may be quite brief or quite extended. This is ideal for occasions when either short or lengthy improvisations are needed, such as in service-playing.

Recommendations

1.   Begin your practice by using Example 9 as a basic plan from which you are free to deviate. Supply the missing voices and invent the content of the empty measures. Write out a full version away from the keyboard; try it out and make any corrections at the keyboard. Then practice the piece; having written out and played your own version will enable you to improvise differing versions with ease. Then practice another version, using only the written outline of Example 9; by now you will know the section themes very well.

2.   Repeat the process above, composing your own questions and designing your own form.

3.   Count aloud as you practice, especially when using the written outline.

4.   You may want to practice, on a daily basis, only one unit or section at a time.

5.   Practice playing the themes and improvising the answers in all four voices, just as we practiced the scales and phrases previously. This will give you enormous skill and equipment for improvising any piece of music.

6.   Practice answers as transitions; then practice transitions as separate entities. Again, pre-determining the length of these transitions is essential. They should balance in length the sections to which they lead. Perhaps a two- or a four-measure transition would balance with an eight-measure section; that transition could be inserted between any of the sections, enabling the improvisor to use keys less closely related to the tonic. Here is an example of a transition as a separate entity that might be inserted between one of the B sections, leading back into one of the A sections:

Example 12

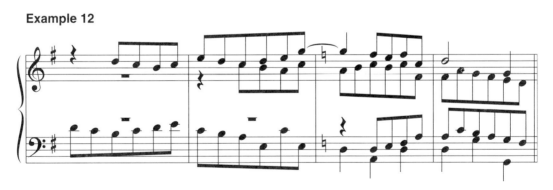

7.   Remember that the eight-measure section is not sacrosanct, nor is the unchanging time signature. Variety adds interest. Our examples are at best over-simplified, and meant as mere starting points.

8.   Develop and refine your song form improvisations so that your service-playing is given greater and more versatile range. Song forms make excellent interludes, preludes, and postludes.

Enjoy creating your own song form, concise or extended.

8. The Sonata Form

At this stage you are more than well equipped to take the song form one step further and create a basic sonatina or a very simple sonata-allegro form. Again, the plan we shall devise will be greatly over-simplified in design, for we shall consider this new project as a rather sophisticated ABA form with a few new elements, such as transitions and episodes, added to connect the major sections of the piece. Elaborations, extensions, and innovations will evolve naturally as you practice this basic form. The basic format we have chosen is not based on any single example in the literature, although later you might want to use a specific piece for your model. Many composers, such as Czerny, Haydn, Schumann, and Vierne, to mention only a few, meticulously followed the dictates of form as organized space.

Again, phrases in units will serve as the essential elements from which the piece will be constructed. We shall then plan an outline using these elements in a manner generally agreed to define and characterize the sonatina or a modestly scaled sonata-allegro form. We will again be practicing and improvising from both written and musical outlines. Here, then, is the written outline, using the key of C minor:

Section	Element	Key	Number of voices	Number of measures	Measures
1. Exposition	Introduction	I	3	4	1–4
	Theme 1	I	4	12	5–16
	Transition	I → V	2	4	17–20
	Theme 2	V	3	9	21–29
				29	
2. Development	Theme 1	V	3	4	30–33
	Bridge/Transition	V → II	2	2	34–35
	Theme 2	II	3	4	36–39
	Bridge/Transition	II → IV	2	2	40–41
	Theme 1 (inverted)	IV	4	4	42–45
	Bridge/Transition	IV → III	2	2	46–47
	Themes 1 and 2 combined	III	4	4	48–51
	Bridge/Transition (sequential)	III → V	3	4	52–55
				26	
3. Recapitulation	Theme 1	I	4	8	56–63
	Bridge/Transition	V	2 (or 3)	2	64–65
	Theme 2	I	3 (or 4)	6	66–71
	Coda	I → VI → IV → V → I	4	4	72–75
				20	
		Grand total:		75	

This plan is obviously quite arbitrary; few if any works in the literature could be so analyzed and reduced to such an elementary scheme. But at least we will begin with a simple, clear-cut outline.

We first compose the two themes, much as we composed question phrases previously. Traditionally themes 1 and 2 serve as major components, heard within the three main divisions of the form; each theme possesses a distinctive musical identity and character, much as did our earlier question phrases. To this end, we will select thematic materials that have strong identities and that provide contrasts in melodic line, rhythm, style, and mood, as in the song forms.

Here is our question for theme 1:

Example 1

Here is our question for theme 2:

Example 2

Here are bridge materials based on theme 1:

Example 3

and on theme 2:

Example 4

These bridge materials are meant to lend unity within contrast, and should therefore be thought of as vital ingredients of the recipe, not merely fillers, despite the term "bridge." Improvising means not filling in, but creating meaningful music, whatever the context or practical function.

Now we are ready for the musical outline (note that not all the bridges/transitions are four measures in length):

Example 5

Example 5 (cont.)

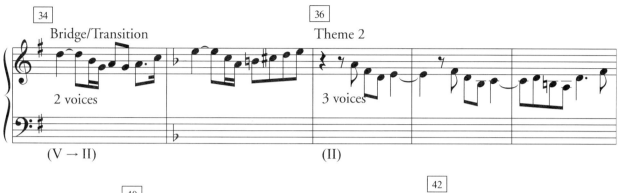

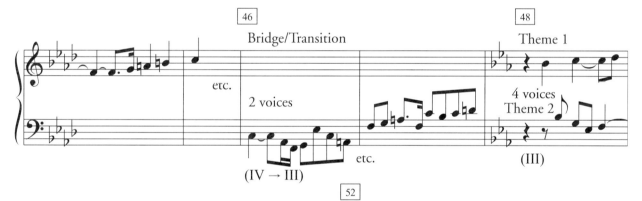

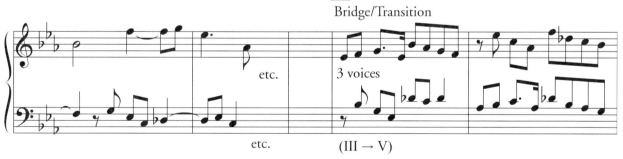

Example 5 (cont.)

There are no markings indicating tempo, dynamic level, expression, phrasing, style, and mood. You will want to experiment with differing sets of markings each time you practice the piece.

The question of theme I is deliberately repeated in measure 13 in order to establish it firmly in the listener's ear.

Note the suggested variations of each theme and the numbers of voices employed at different times within each section, all of which should heighten musical interest through variety of thematic contour and texture.

Note the several registers given to thematic and bridge materials, which are passed from voice to voice. We thereby enrich the construction with differing timbres.

Bridges and episodes may be thought of as closely related answers to whatever precedes their appearances.

Recommendations

1. Begin your practice by using Example 5, supplying the missing voices and empty measures. Write out a full version away from the keyboard; try it out, make corrections, and then practice it. Begin with the musical outline and then move to the written outline; by then you will know the thematic material very well.

2. Repeat the process above, composing your own themes, altering the composition of the structure to suit your individual plans. Be careful to keep the sections balanced in relation to each other; as always, the planning and control of space is essential.

3. Count aloud as you practice, especially when improvising from the written outline.

4. As with the song forms, practicing the piece in units (just as we practice the repertoire) is strongly urged. For example, you might begin by working out the exposition one day, the recapitulation the following day, and the development the next two days. You might use the same process for the smaller segments, such as themes, bridges, and episodes.

5. Remember that Example 5 is but the merest suggestion for a start. You will want to vary the lengths of each phrase and each section, distributing your own themes among the various voices as you wish. Also, try different keys in differing orders.

9. The Toccata

Toccatas appear in many guises, forms, and configurations for the keyboard, ranging from the suave elegance of Frescobaldi to the sonic brilliance of Sokola. We will plan a toccata that is built, in a general way, upon models from the late nineteenth and early twentieth centuries, decidedly French in style. Emphasis will be placed upon the practicing, growth, and development of finger dexterity; we will work primarily at being able to play figurations at rapid tempos in both hands over a cantus firmus, choosing one or more of the styles of the hymn prelude mastered earlier.

Let us begin with the organ hymn prelude form. We will make quite elaborate the patterns played on the manuals and superimposed over the cantus firmus in the pedals or bass part (Chap. 6, Ex. 3), which will be the tune "Nun danket alle Gott":

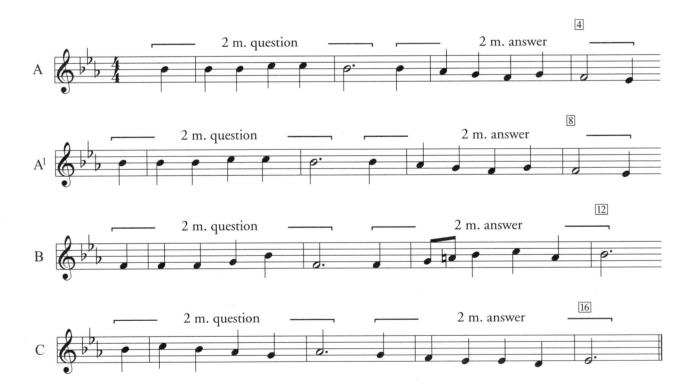

1. Practice one-on-one parallel intervals of quarter-note value in the right hand with the pedal. Of the several intervals available to us, we will arbitrarily choose the interval of a perfect fourth:

Example 1

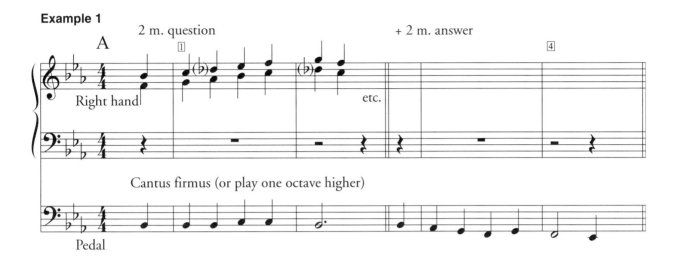

2. Practice one-on-one parallel intervals of quarter-note value in the left hand with the pedal. We will choose the interval of a perfect fifth, because it gives color and mild dissonances when heard with the perfect fourths of the right hand later, and because it will make organizing the figurations for each hand easier in these initial stages of practicing:

Example 2

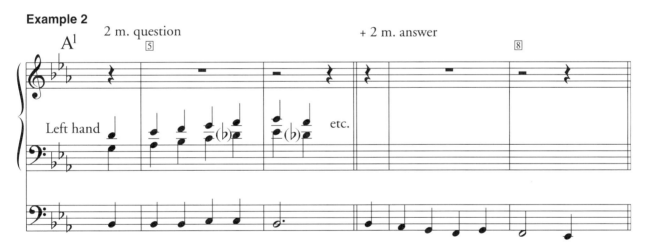

In order to avoid digital confusion in this early stage of our practicing, we should use the same set of fingers for all intervals, such as fingers 1 or 2 and 5 in each hand, or whichever combination is most comfortable and reliable. Without finger substitutions, the result will be non-legato, which is perfectly acceptable, although it may prove a somewhat new experience for many organists who hitherto have tried to achieve a perfect legato. As in our early scale and phrase improvisations (Chap. 2, Ex. 51), we keep the intervals moving in scalewise progressions, without skips. As we attain greater skill, skips will naturally suggest themselves; however, in this early stage, skipping about can cause great confusion in deciding, first, where to skip to, and, second, how to maintain the intervals while the skip is being made.

   3. Practice both hands together in quarter-note values, separated by the interval of a third (major or minor). Here is a written outline of this configuration:

Right hand [Perfect fourth
  Interval ↕ Major or minor third
Left hand [Perfect fifth

   Here is the musical outline:

Example 3

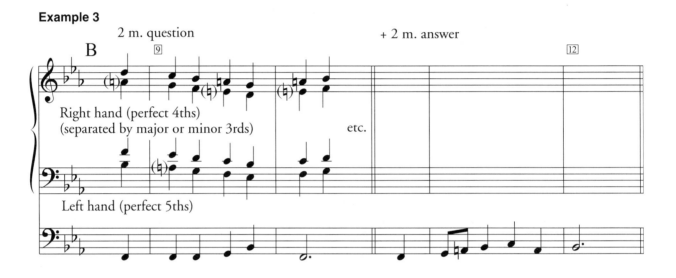

Right hand (perfect 4ths)
(separated by major or minor 3rds)   etc.

Left hand (perfect 5ths)

   Practice without the pedal until you gain sufficient confidence to add the cantus firmus. (Practicing each hand separately for long series of consecutive intervals is most helpful in acquiring this technique.)

   4. Practice both hands together, but alternate hands in eighth-note values so that a two-on-one pattern results. We will maintain at all times the interval of a major or minor third that separates the two hands, lest we lose control of the figurations in each hand later on. We are at liberty to observe or disregard the key signature in determining the nature of the intervals in each hand (the alternate versions are shown as accidentals in parentheses on the staves). Note that, to heighten interest and define contour, we now tend to move the parallel intervals in motion contrary to that of the cantus firmus.

Example 4

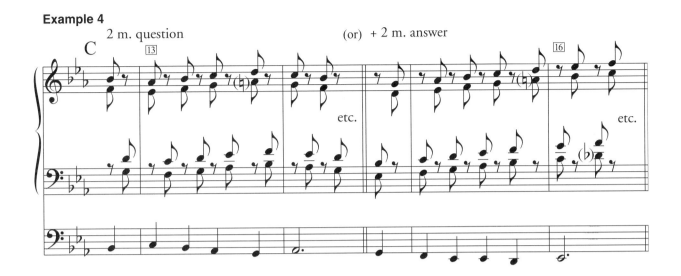

5. *Practice first hands separately and then together, but alternating all of the notes of each interval in each hand in sixteenth-note values so as to produce a four-on-one pattern:*

Example 5

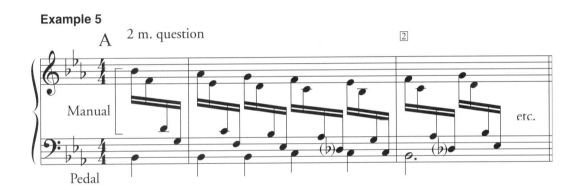

Remember that, once the technique in each stage is mastered, the pedals should be added.

6. *Practice a new configuration in which the interval between the hands becomes a major or minor tenth* (which is, of course, that same interval of a major or minor third, plus an octave). Here is a written outline of this configuration.

Right hand		Perfect fourth
	Interval ↕	Major or minor tenth
Left hand		Perfect fifth

Here is the musical outline of this configuration, one-on-one, in quarter notes:

Example 6

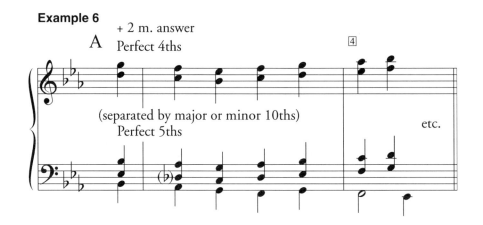

A + 2 m. answer
Perfect 4ths

(separated by major or minor 10ths)
Perfect 5ths

etc.

alternating the hands, two-on-one, in eighth notes:

Example 7

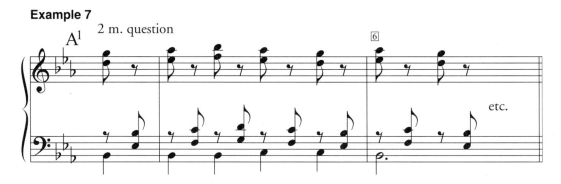

A¹ 2 m. question

etc.

alternating the hands, four-on-one, in sixteenth notes:

Example 8

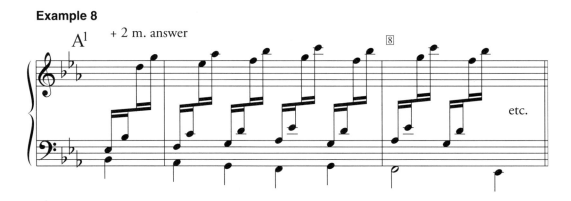

A¹ + 2 m. answer

etc.

As always, we practice hands separately, then hands together, then hands and pedal together.

    7. Practice this configuration by adding an octave to match the top note of the right hand and an octave to match the bottom note of the left hand. Here is the written outline:

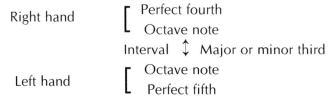

Right hand   ⌈ Perfect fourth
               ⌊ Octave note
Interval   ↕   Major or minor third
Left hand   ⌈ Octave note
               ⌊ Perfect fifth

The interval separating the hands is now a major or minor third.
Here is the musical outline, one-on-one in quarter notes:

Example 9

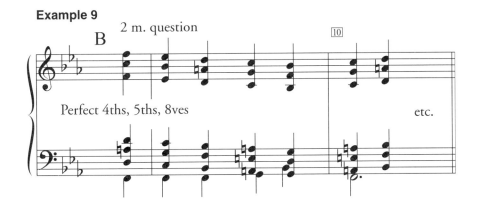

8. *Alternate hands, two-on-one in eighth notes (or repeated, four-on-one in sixteenth notes):*

Example 10

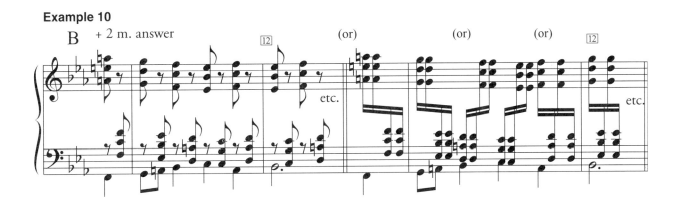

four-on-one in sixteenth notes:

Example 11

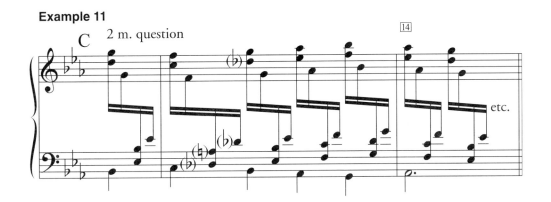

and six-on-one in sixteenth-note triplets:

Example 12

Note how many patterns of alternating these notes are available to us.

9. Practice an extended version of this configuration by adding an extra note between each hand's interval notes and octave notes. Here is the written outline:

Right hand
- (♪) Top note
- (♪) Perfect fourth lower
- (♪) One note lower
- (♪) Octave note below

(answered by)

Left hand
- (♪) Bottom note
- (♪) Perfect fifth above
- (♪) One note higher
- (♪) Octave note above

Here is the musical outline of this configuration, six-on-one in sixteenth-note triplets (with the perfect fourths and fifths played together and the other notes played separately):

Example 13

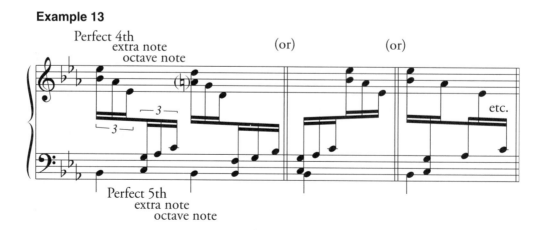

eight-on-one in thirty-second notes (with each of the four notes in each hand played separately):

Example 14

and sixteen-on-one in sixty-fourth notes, created by merely repeating any given pattern:

Example 15

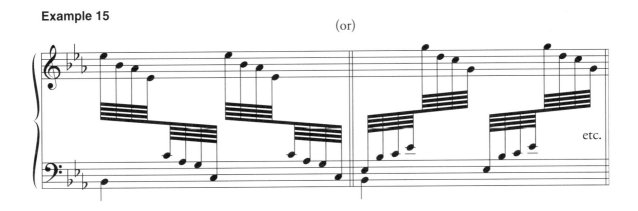

The patterns within these configurations can be varied in an infinite number of ways.

As another form for our toccata we may use the interpolation prelude (you may want to refer to the outlines of Chap. 6, Ex. 4). The introduction, interpolation, and coda/epilogue sections are merely figurations built on the answer to each of the phrases within each section.

Note that the number of measures is different in "Nun danket alle Gott" (2 mm. q + 2 mm. a), but the form, in terms of proportion, remains the same. Depending upon which figuration you choose, the introduction might be improvised as in Chap. 6, Ex. 4 (based on the question of the final phrase section of the cantus firmus):

Example 16

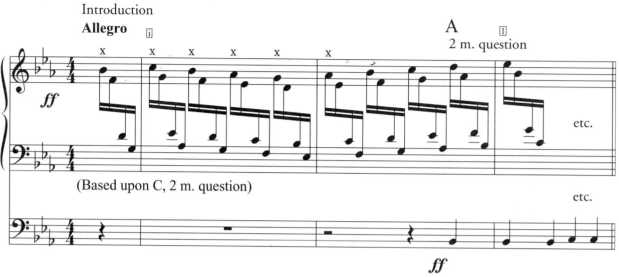

the first interpolation might be improvised as follows (based on the answer of the A phrase section of the tune):

Example 17

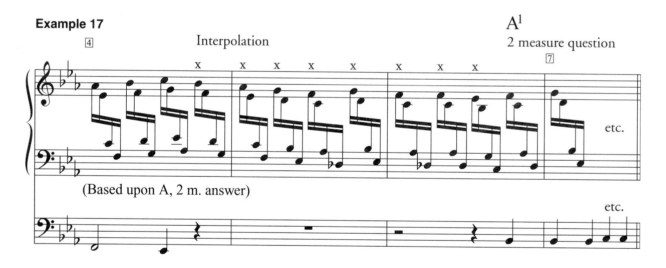

and a rather grand coda/epilogue might be improvised after the final interpolation (based on the question of the A and the A^1 phrase sections of the cantus firmus):

Example 18

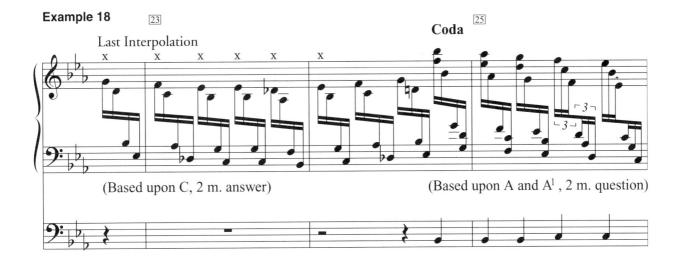

Last Interpolation

(Based upon C, 2 m. answer)   (Based upon A and A¹, 2 m. question)

Our practice method remains the same: write a non-musical and then a musical outline; practice first from the latter and then the former, counting aloud as you improvise.

Note that the different structures of various hymn tunes will oblige us to make appropriate spatial adjustments, especially in the interpolations.

At this stage we will want to minimize the number of notes in our musical outlines; they should now be thought of as cues, notated for purposes of visualization.

The intervals from which the figurations evolve have been arbitrarily chosen for purposes of illustration. Virtually any set of intervals will serve as well, especially those most comfortable under the individual's hands. The important idea is to maintain the chosen intervals throughout the initial stages of practice. As the technique is mastered, variation will suggest itself.

Recommendations

1. Practice very long series of parallel intervals and figurations in each hand, perhaps fifty to seventy measures at a time, so as to gain dexterity and build finger memory for these patterns. Keep the same fingering throughout, especially in the early stages.

2. Don't grow impatient in acquiring these considerable digital skills: slow practice is of the essence. Think of it as an investment that will pay many dividends in the years to come. Certainly we must practice this style of music from the literature slowly in order to achieve maximum benefit; remember that we should practice our own improvisations in exactly the same manner as the formal compositions of others.

3. The cantus firmus need not be plain and unadorned at all times, but should be made more elaborate through ornamentation. In fact, depending on the nature of the configurations you have chosen for the hands, you might wish to bring the cantus firmus to greater prominence by playing it in octaves on the pedalboard.

Above all, enjoy the challenge of improvising an exciting toccata on virtually any tune of your choosing. Needless to say, you will create quite an impact at the conclusion of a recital or service.

10. The Canon

The canon is one of the more intriguing, challenging, and rewarding of all the contrapuntal forms, requiring no less concentration than the other improvisatory forms we have already encountered. In fact, improvising a canon is rather like solving a crossword puzzle, in that the instances in which the independent lines coincide provide the hinges upon which the canon moves.

We will begin very simply with a canonic scheme of which Franck was an undisputed master, and which abounds within the corpus of his works for varied instruments and ensembles; one of his hallmarks is what we shall call the *stop and start canon*. The leader voice makes a statement and then becomes motionless while the follower voice repeats that statement; then the leader makes another statement, the follower remaining motionless in turn; and so on. Here is a written outline of this scheme, with the follower (Voice 2) repeating the statement at one measure's distance:

	M. 1	M. 2	M. 3	M. 4	
Voice 1	Active	Passive	Active	Passive	
					Etc.
Voice 2	—	Active	Passive	Active	

or

	M. 1	M. 2	M. 3	M. 4	
Voice 1 ¾	♩ ♩ ♩	♩.	♩ ♩. ♪	♩ ♩	
					Etc.
Voice 2 ¾	‐	♩ ♩ ♩	♩.	♩ ♩. ♪	

If we want a canon with little if any dissonance, we will be ever mindful, first, of the initial beat of each measure, and, second, of the content of the active measures. In other words, we must always think at least one measure ahead, in anticipation of what the resulting music will sound like when active and passive lines coincide.

Here is a musical outline of this sort of canon at the octave, with one measure's remove between follower and leader voices:

Example 1

Note that the interval between the voices on the first beat of each measure is consonant.

Canons of this ilk need not remain tonally static in order to sound consonant; by the simple use of tones consonant with one another, modulations are easily effected. By measure 5, we have begun to leave the tonic key, arriving at the submediant in measure 6, the mediant in measure 7, the dominant key in measure 8, and are on our way to B minor as early as measure 9. Let us carry this idea further by continuing our musical outline:

Example 2

Note the use of enharmonic notes to facilitate our moving into and out of several keys (another famous trademark of Franck's). Note also that we have improvised a piece of some twenty-four measures' duration, a length well known to us from our phrase and song form improvisations.

We will now organize our practice of this canon by designing an ABA song form (Chap. 7, Ex. 3), based on the hymn tune "Picardy":

Here is the non-musical outline for a canon in this form in a minor key:

A	I	(tonic)	8 mm.	(perhaps 4 m. q + 4 m. a)
B	VI	(parallel major)	8 mm.	(perhaps 4 m. q + 4 m. a)
A¹	I		9 mm.	(perhaps 4 m. q + 4 m. a + final m.)

and a musical outline:

Example 3

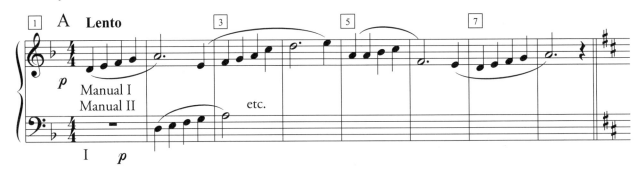

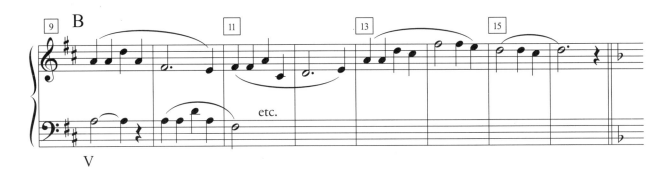

The ninth measure in A¹ (measure 25) is necessary in order to accommodate the follower's ending.

In A¹, measures that previously would have been passive have now grown restless and evolved into greater activity.

Only fragments of "Picardy" have been selected for thematic treatment here. We need not feel pressed to treat a melody in a literal or strict manner or in its entirety, but rather may adapt recognizable patterns derived from the original melody. With such a flexible approach, virtually any tune may be developed as a canon.

The follower measures have been left empty so that you can practice by following the leader voice. You will want to practice the same outline, reversing clefs and hands. Another useful way to practice this sort of canon is to enlist the participation of a friend to practice with you, each taking turns at improvising first the leader and then the follower.

We can now improvise a simple accompaniment, consisting of parallel intervals in one hand, the leader in the other hand, and the follower in the pedals, as illustrated in the following musical outline:

Example 4

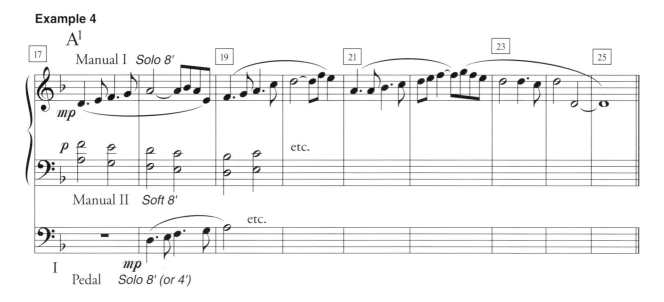

Here is an outline of the same plan, except that the pedal now takes the part of the leader, the left hand the follower, and the parallel intervals have been expanded to a chain of first-inversion chords in the right hand:

Example 5

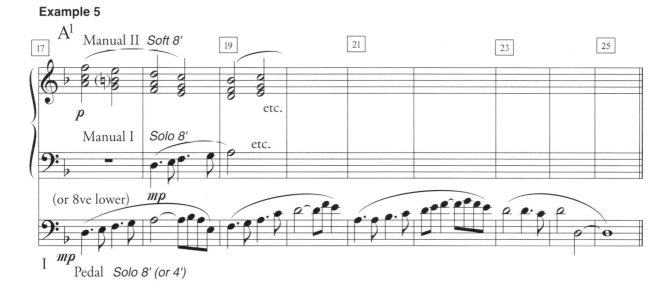

In both outlines the movement of the succession of parallel intervals has been stepwise. In this way we avoid, in this initial phase, potential confusion caused by skips.

Although our canons have been placed at the octave, they would work just as well at the unison. You might want to experiment with different ranges (and perhaps with different registrations at the organ) to provide contrast.

Once the octave/unison canons have been accomplished, you might want to take this process an additional step by having the follower answer the leader at another interval, as in this outline, in which the interval is a tenth:

Example 6

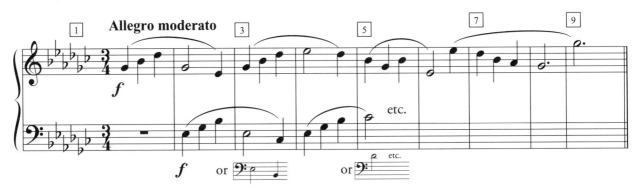

The leader stays within a pentatonic range, a safe way to avoid much dissonance. The practicing is further facilitated in this early phase by the leader's remaining exclusively on the black keys.

Note that, in order also to avoid dissonance, the melody in the follower has been altered occasionally by a half or whole step (measures 3 and 5); this may be done freely, as the ear dictates. Canons need not be strict, especially if one wants the follower to remain in the same or original key.

We will now take our improvisation one step further still, creating a canon in three voices. We will give the first follower the interval of a tenth and the second follower a thirteenth:

Example 7

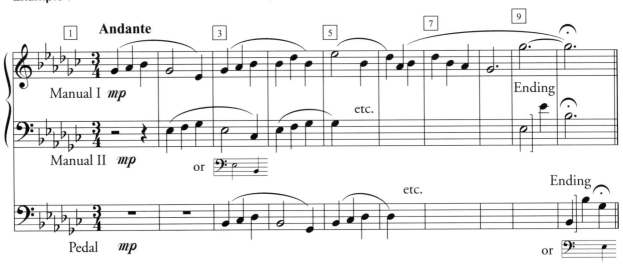

There are likely to be intervallic alterations at several points along the way, in order to accommodate a sense of key. Thus it is important to maintain strictly the rhythmic character of each voice, as compensation.

Note that this plan may be practiced initially at the octave or unison, as before.

These examples are but simple suggestions for the beginner. Many possibilities await the improviser who masters the concept and who will then want to improvise more sophisticated canons. Remember also that many composers, such as Franck and Vierne, have shown us how canons may provide wonderfully contrasting sections within the song and sonata forms, among others, that we have already learned to improvise.

Recommendations

1. Practice the canon in much the same manner in which we have practiced all the preceding forms. First, practice from the musical outline; learn to supply the follower's voice by first writing out those lines and then playing them. Second, learn to supply the voices from the uncompleted outline. Third, write your own leader voice, practicing it in the same way.

2. In the three-voice canon exercises, practice but two voices at a time. You might start with the leader and the first follower only; then the leader and the second follower only; then the two followers only. When beginning the practice of three-voice canons, you might do well to keep them at intervals of a unison or octave.

3. Practice canons with the answers both less and more than a measure's distance apart; this will extend your concentration and focus.

4. Consult, analyze, and learn from the masters of the form, such as Purcell, Bach, Mendelssohn, Franck, and Dupré.

11. The Duo and the Trio

As with several of the forms previously discussed, the terms duo and trio have had different meanings and styles throughout the course of music history. A duo, to us, will mean simply a two-voice improvisation with a soprano part that performs the melody or cantus firmus, with a bass voice in either imitation or support. A trio will designate a three-voice improvisation with the top and the middle voices each featuring the thematic material, usually in an imitative fashion, while the bottom voice chiefly supports and occasionally imitates one or both of the other voices. We shall rely upon models from the master, Bach, although many more exist in the works of such composers as Brahms, Rheinberger, and Distler, to mention but a few. These challenging forms may prove difficult for some at first, but they can provide opportunities for innovation and growth within a highly disciplined framework.

1. Design a duo based on a hymn tune, the basic form of which we will derive from Bach's two-part inventions. Our version will be not an exact copy of any single invention but rather an amalgamation of several. There will be but two elements at work here: a subject, based upon the first two measures of "Easter Hymn":

Example 1

and material of great simplicity in the nature of a countersubject to accompany the subject each time it appears. Sequences will evolve from both these elements.

Here is a non-musical outline of our duo, with the Roman numerals denoting the keys and the arrows improvised countersubject materials, ("motion" arrows indicate a transition to another key):

Measure Numbers:	1	2	3	4
Voice 1:	Subject (I)	→	Subject (V)	→
Voice 2:	— — —	Subject (I)	→	Subject (V)

Measure Numbers:	5	6	7	8
Voice 1:	Sequence ⟹	Sequence ⟹	Sequence ⟹	Sequence to Cadence
Voice 2:	Sequence ⟹	Sequence ⟹	Sequence ⟹	Sequence to Cadence

Measure Numbers:	9	10	11	12
Voice 1:	→	Subject (V)	→	Subject (II)
Voice 2:	Subject (V)	→	Subject (II)	→

Measure Numbers:	13	14	15	16
Voice 1:	Sequence ⟹	Sequence ⟹	Subject (VI)	→
Voice 2:	Sequence ⟹	Sequence ⟹	→	Subject (VI)

Measure Numbers:	17	18	19	20
Voice 1:	Subject (II)	→	Sequence ⟹	Sequence ⟹
Voice 2:	→	Subject (II)	Sequence ⟹	Sequence ⟹

Measure Numbers:	21	22	23	24
Voice 1:	→	Subject (I)	Sequence ⟹	Final
Voice 2:	Subject (V)	→	Sequence ⟹	Cadence ⟹

Note the progression of keys: from tonic to dominant, to supertonic (the minor dominant of the dominant), to submediant (the minor dominant of the supertonic), back to the supertonic, dominant, and tonic. These keys are, of course, very closely related, and pose no modulatory problems.

Note the balance provided by the four sets of sequences; they afford relief from the subject during its absence while allowing it prominence when it returns.

Here is a musical outline of our duo:

Example 2

Example 2 (cont.)

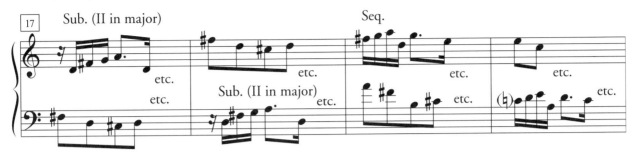

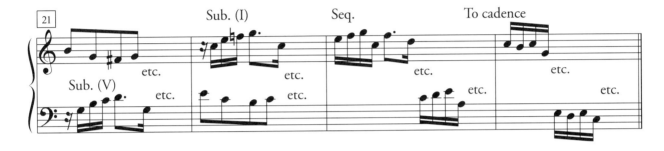

Note that the two elements of subject and countersubject have been used consistently throughout this example, as have the sequential materials (based upon the third and fourth measures of "Easter Hymn"). In the initial stages of your practicing, you may want to restrict yourself thus, in order to control your primary materials at all times. As you progress you will feel more free to experiment, especially with different sequential materials.

Sequences are of invaluable help in modulating. Note how only the slightest alteration of this very simple sequence can lead us in entirely different directions:

Example 3

Sequences are easy to plan and delightful to practice, for their many options can easily lead us to exotic tonal destinations and return us home just as efficiently. There are virtually unlimited numbers of sequence patterns awaiting your discovery. Given their brevity, they are easy to work into almost any practice schedule, so that eventually they are improvised as if by second nature. Sequences can provide musical bridges in almost any form, especially the contrapuntal ones.

Our practice plan remains basically the same as before. We will first practice from the musical outline, writing in the missing notes and then checking them at the keyboard; next we will practice from the outline without the added notes; and finally we will use the written outline. You will want to design your own duo in exactly the same way: compose a subject of strong melodic and rhythmic character (which may or may not be based on an existing melody—you will, in any case, eventually want to compose your own subject); then compose the countersubject materials for the sequences. All of this should be done on staff paper, but with as few notes as possible, so that you will improvise more and more using the empty measures. You will be pleasantly surprised to learn how quickly you will internalize and memorize the main materials; you will begin to find yourself writing out fewer and fewer notes and improvising without them more. As this skill is perfected, you will eventually discover that you need no paper at all before you, for you will have completely digested the form and mastered improvising within it. This phenomenon applies, by extension, to everything we have studied and practiced up to this point. Again, there is no mystique or magic to improvising, just consistent and conscientious practice.

2. *Design a trio based on our work in the duo.* The non-musical outline remains the same in terms of structure; what differs is the addition of a bass line that will support the upper two. We might think of this construction in historical terms: two solo voices or instruments supported by a basso continuo (a flute and violin supported by a cello, for example). Our musical outline will not suggest countersubject or sequential materials except in our new bass part; having mastered such elements in the duo improvisations, we will now concentrate on improvising the added bass line that will give harmonic underpinning to our trio.

Example 4

Example 4 (cont.)

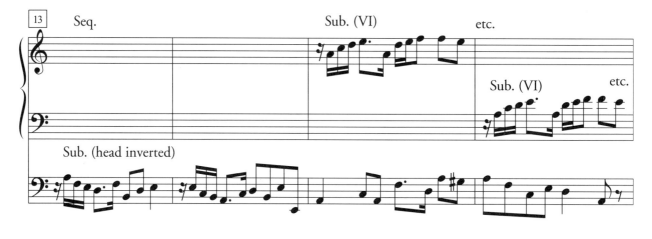

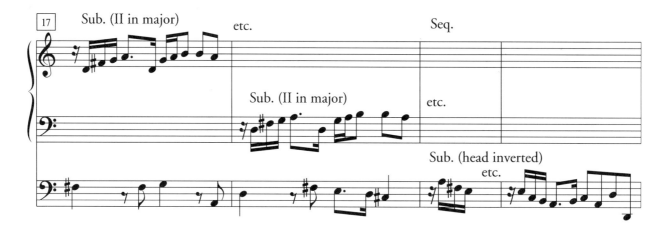

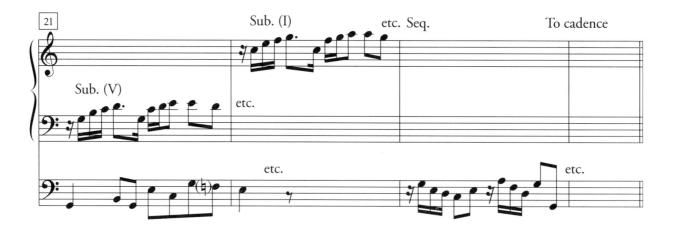

Note the use of inversion in the bass-line sequences (measures 5–6, 13–14, 19–20).

We may now practice sequences in which all three parts are involved, answering one another. Here is a musical outline of such a sequence, using materials from measure 5 of our duo:

Example 5

and a sequence using the materials from measure 5 of our trio:

Example 6

Again, these examples are the simplest of suggestions; many more ideas will occur to you as your practicing continues. For example, a subject may be ripe for inversion in statement or response.

Effort should be made to create as much contrary motion as possible within the two solo voices and, whenever possible, between them and the bass voice; this general approach almost always produces interesting counterpoint.

Recommendations

1. Practice your duo at first without imitation, playing the subject in the top voice accompanied by a very simple bass line. Then play the subject in the bass voice, accompanied by an obbligato or descant-like improvisation in the top voice. (We have mastered this technique in our scale and phrase improvisations.) Eventually the secondary voice will want to imitate the subject; at this point, measure by measure or section by section, you may begin to develop your skills further by using first the musical and then the non-musical outline. Presently the whole piece will begin to take shape and fall into place.

2. Counting aloud as you play is still an invaluable and helpful device.

3. For both duo and trio, use the musical outline first, practicing each hand separately; then do the same using the non-musical outline. For the trio you will want to practice each line separately and then in pairs—top voice and middle voice, top voice and bass voice, middle voice and bass voice—until each voice is securely independent and controlled.

4. After successful practicing of these elements, you will want to design your own non-musical outline (followed, of course, by its musical version), refashioning the form—indeed, creating your own. These might be simpler and briefer, or more complex and extended, depending on how you choose to adapt the basic ideas. As always, the intellect guides the performer; writing before playing is the secret of all improvising. If your ideas are meticulously organized and your practice procedures carefully followed, your improvising will be convincing and compelling.

5. No restrictions regarding the particular styles of duo and trio are implied in the examples given here; they certainly need not be Baroque in character. They are merely suggestions, and could easily have been written in a different historical idiom. Our purpose here is to provide a working structure; but within that particular structure, as we have pointed out before, there is no "correct" way to improvise. For example, imagine how intriguing it would be to improvise a duo or trio in which each voice is in a different key!

12. The Fugue

Few musical forms and structures fascinate the musician as much as the fugue. A fugue sums up the contrapuntal possibilities inherent in other forms, forming one complete entity from many related elements and parts. We have already mastered several elements that will now serve us well as we, too, sum up our acquired and accumulated improvisational skills.

Certainly, counterpoint is present in all good part-writing, harmonization, and rhythmic organization. But when we began our work on the point-of-imitation hymn prelude form, we were actually improvising fugal entries when we practiced the points of imitation themselves. You will recall that one subject was stated in the tonic, then answered in the dominant, which in turn was followed by a reiteration in a third voice back in the tonic, and so on. Mastering the canon enhanced our contrapuntal technique through creation of the follower, which answered the leader (or subject). We further expanded our skills in the duo and trio, in which we learned to develop a subject and answer it in another voice, all in different keys. Further, we learned to improvise sequences or connecting passages (episodes). Clearly, we have acquired almost all the basic equipment we shall need for improvising a fugue.

At the same time, we need to realize that a working knowledge of counterpoint, with the attendant "rules" that have come down to us through the many eras of Western musical creativity, will give us a sure and firm foundation upon which to improvise. Here we are well advised to consult with such composer/teachers as Professor Kennan (see the Bibliography).

As usual, we discover, in choosing models upon which to base our design of the form, that there are many different kinds of fugues; they appear in all sizes, shapes, and styles. We will settle on a structure that, more often than not, one finds in fugues of the eighteenth and nineteenth centuries.

Here we have a subject (an extended version of our duo and trio subjects) as the main event, accompanied by a countersubject, especially throughout the course of the first section (or exposition) of the fugue. We will attempt to build the connecting passages or bridges (episodes) upon thematic materials derived from the subject and countersubject. We will think of our fugue as consisting primarily of three major sections:

I.   Exposition
II. Extra entries (or development) of the subject
III. Final entries (or recapitulation) of the subject

As we have already learned, we should design first and foremost the overall structure, as always greatly oversimplifying the form in our first attempt. Our modest design will suggest the shorter fugues of such diverse composers as Bach, Mendelssohn, Brahms, Saint-Saëns and Dupré. Here, then, is a written outline for improvising a fugue in four voices:

Section	Voice	Key	Number of voices	Number of measures	Measures
I. Exposition					
Subject	Soprano	I	1	4	1–4
Answer	Alto	V	2	4	5–8
(Soprano becomes countersubject)					
Episode	Soprano and alto	V → I	2	2	9–10
Subject	Tenor	I	3	4	11–14
(Alto becomes countersubject)					
Answer	Bass	V	4	4	15–18
(Tenor becomes countersubject)					
Episode to cadence	All	V	4	2	19–20
II. Extra entries/Development					
Episode	Alto and tenor	V → II	2	2	21–22
Subject	Bass	II	3	4	23–26
Episode	Tenor and bass	II → VI	2	2	27–28
Subject	Soprano	VI (major)	3	4	29–32
Answer	Tenor	III	3	4	33–36
Episode	Tenor and soprano	III → V	2	2	37–38
Subject	Alto	V	2	4	39–42
Episode	Soprano, alto, and tenor	V → I	3	2	43–44
III. Final entries/Recapitulation					
Subject	Bass (in augmentation)	I	1	6	45–51
Answer	Tenor (over bass)	V	2	4	46–49
Answer	Alto (over bass and tenor)	VI	3	4	47–50
Subject	Soprano (over bass, tenor, and alto)	I	4	4	48–51
Coda	All to final cadence	I	4	4	51–54

Note that, in the exposition, the voice that is the subject or the answer becomes, as if by metamorphosis, the countersubject against which the next voice enters. Also note that in the Final entries/Recapitulation, the tenor and alto answers and the soprano subject all overlap each other over the bass in augmentation in measures 46–48.

Having now designed the structure of our fugue, with specific attention to space (numbers of measures), modulations, textures (number and combination of voices employed at any given moment), and appearances of the subject and countersubject, we are now ready to compose that subject and its countersubject, based on the hymn tune "Dix":

We will naturally be most interested in the first few measures of the tune as we prepare to compose the subject. We could easily use the first four measures of the tune exactly as written; we could also alter it slightly:

Example 1

or considerably:

Example 2

or extensively:

Example 3

or radically:

Example 4

Note the seemingly unlimited number of ways in which the tune may be treated. We will choose features from each of these five versions in creating our subject, taking care to give it a very strong character with interesting rhythmic features and contour of line:

Example 5

Note that we have reversed the order of the F# and A as they originally appeared in measure 1 of the tune.

We will want to practice our subject starting on every scale degree of the tonic key, with each hand and then the pedals separately. This helps us to memorize and internalize the subject, so that it falls totally under our control.

In creating the countersubject, we will want to think in terms of material that will provide contrast with our subject, which is rhythmically energetic and somewhat angular in shape. The major purpose of the countersubject is to cast a spotlight onto the subject, as it were, drawing attention to it and throwing it into bold relief. We see at once that the first measure of the tune will again give us what we are searching for. We may also quote from the third measure of the phrase, attaching these two fragments together in order to accompany the more complex subject:

Example 6

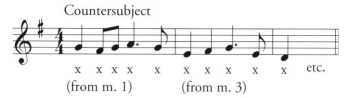

We will first want to practice the countersubject alone, beginning on each note of the tonic scale, as we did with the subject, and then together with the subject in the same manner. Thus the two basic elements of the fugue will become completely assimilated, both mentally and digitally. In practicing the subject and countersubject together, we begin in the dominant key:

Example 7

and then move to the tonic key:

Example 8

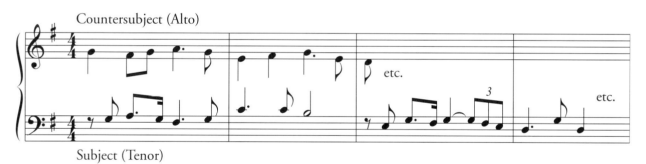

We may search through the remainder of the tune for materials that may be used in the episodes if necessary. We see at once that the third phrase, in measures 9 and 10 of the tune (or the B section of this AAB song form) provides us with such material. We may supply various patterns for use in sequences within the episodes:

Example 9

We will want to practice all episode materials on each note of the tonic scale, as before.

We are now fully prepared and ready to practice our fugue; here is the musical outline:

Example 10

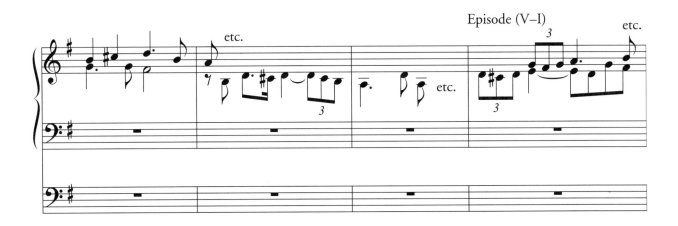

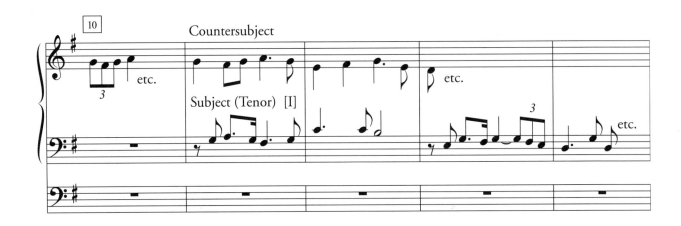

Example 10 (cont.)

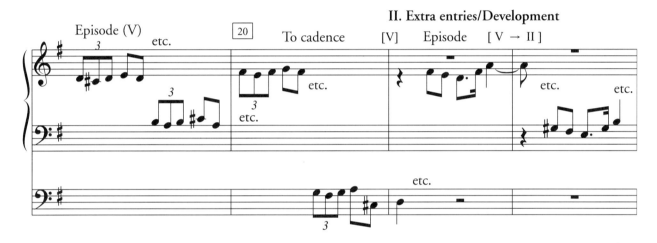

II. Extra entries/Development

Example 10 (cont.)

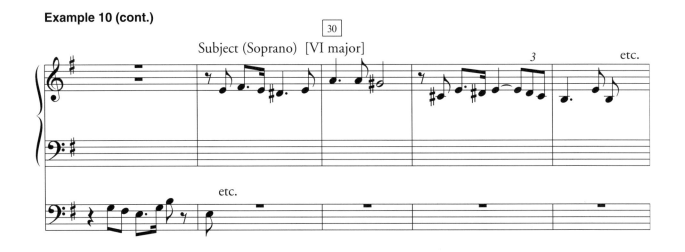

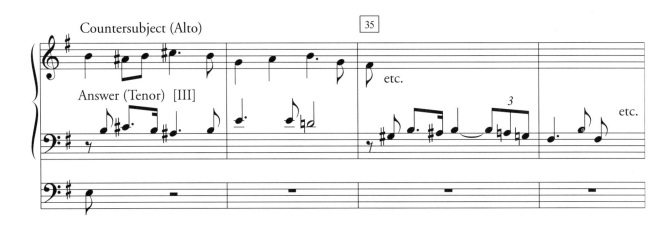

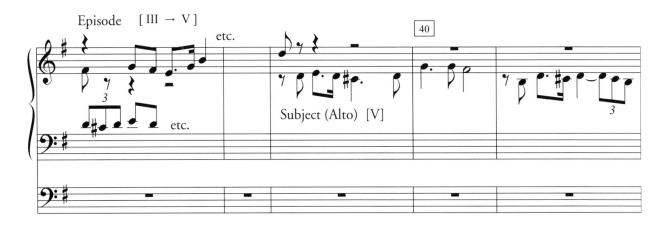

Example 10 (cont.)

Note that all notations, terms, and numbers correspond precisely with those of the non-musical outline.

The countersubject always accompanies the subject (except in its initial statement, of course) and answer throughout the exposition; traditionally, this is essential in the formal composition of a fugue. Thereafter, however, the countersubject need not accompany the subject; in our fugue, it does so only once (measures 33–34).

Our practice procedure will remain the same as before, improvising in exactly the same way that we practice keyboard literature. First, we supply the missing notes in the musical outline, completing the fugue voice by voice and measure by measure. Second, using this outline, we practice our fugue section by section, beginning with each voice separately, then in pairs (hands together, right hand and pedal, left hand and pedal), and then—only when each of these phases is completely and confidently mastered—all together, keeping a very slow tempo at first and carefully increasing it in easy unhurried stages. As in learning keyboard literature, slow practice is time consuming, but the effort is repaid many times over in secure mastery of the piece. Third, we practice the fugue using the written outline. Last, we repeat the process, composing our own subject freely or deriving it from another existing tune.

Recommendations

1. As our fugue has been planned arbitrarily, you will want eventually to change and refine the outlines in accordance with your preferences and taste. Our version does not pretend to be definitive (much less "correct"), but rather an example from which to learn.

2. Although our fugue was constructed in three sections, it may easily be expanded. Here, by way of example, is the barest outline of a fugue containing five sections:

	Section	Length/Space
I.	Exposition	20–30 mm.
II.	Extra entries	12–20 mm.
III.	Extra entries, but similar to the formal construction of the exposition probably in a different key	12–20 or 30 mm.
IV.	Extra entries	12–20 mm.
V.	Final entries	12–20 mm.

This plan will result in an extensive but well-organized development section that allows much greater range and space, as well as increased possibilities for modulation and textural contrasts.

3. We have dealt mainly with the basic elements of a conventional fugue, but also have incorporated three of the more sophisticated aspects: inversion, augmentation, and the number of voices employed. Others, such as tonal answers, diminutions, and even double fugue, will suggest themselves as you continue to practice and grow, expanding all the many features of the form.

Coda

You are now a skilled *improvisateur*. You are a greater musician than you were before. Your range of musical expression is much larger than it was before you began to improvise. A fertile and unlimited field of creativity is yours to tend and cultivate.

You may not feel confident about improvising a sonata or a fugue, at least in public, but you have worked hard to acquire the skills that will enable you to master these and other forms. In fact, you will eventually adapt and transform these suggested musical structures into your own personalized versions. This creative process validates your means of music-making. *You* have become the creator, identified by your unique style, which will continue to evolve and transform itself as you continue to work and grow. As we have seen, variation, elaboration, and derivation suggest themselves as your curiosity is stimulated by the repetitive nature of practicing.

We are all occasionally stumped by problems for which there seem no solutions. Don't be discouraged. Try going back to the previous step and continue to refine it. You will find it easier to move forward again, and that difficult problem will probably suggest its own solutions. Trust your musical instinct.

In our enthusiasm to create music, we often attempt too much at once, which is rather like trying to play a demanding and difficult composition up to tempo before it is ready to perform. If we must err (and err we will, from time to time), let it be on the spare rather than the extravagant side.

I well recall a Sunday service many years ago on a warm July morning during which we were scheduled to sing "The Star-Spangled Banner." I alerted the choir that I would be giving that piece the "treatment" (a term that I rather like and had learned from a young chorister, and which refers to re-harmonizing or improvising a "free" hymn accompaniment). The great moment arrived and, after a brief interlude that included an unsophisticated fanfare, we launched into the patriotic piece. After the octaves of the opening phrase, I began to elaborate: "by the dawn's early light" found a deceptive cadence; "the twilight's last gleaming" revealed passing tones and a few neighboring notes. Stops were added "through the perilous fight"; there were "gallantly streaming" alternate chords. A full swell's "red glare" led to "the bombs' bursting in air." More passing tones, chromatic this time, led to resulting alternate chords and "our flag was still there." "That star-spangled" seventh chord (or was it a ninth chord?) did indeed "yet wave" beneath the descant of an added fifth voice; a marching bass with full pedal propelled us "o'er the land of the free." Surprising—if not shocking—harmonies, with full organ, were resolved as, at last, we were back to the tonic of "the home of the brave." The congregation's singing increased in volume commensurate with all the goings-on at the console. We all ended together, despite all the musical distractions that I, carried away, had so generously provided.

My dear mother-in-law, visiting us at the time, was a very musical person and a very gentle lady. At lunch after the service, she leaned toward me and said happily, "Gerre, it was so wonderful to sing our national anthem in church today."

Expecting to be stroked, I responded eagerly, "Well, it really was fun, wasn't it?"

Warmly and sincerely she replied, "Yes, it was." There was a pause, and then, more serious, she asked with genuine curiosity, "By the way, what were *you* playing?"

With all my youthful ardor and dedication to my craft, I had almost succeeded, by doing too much too soon, in destroying the congregation's contribution to the service. The moral of this story is that we must strive to maintain that delicate balance required by art between virtuosity and good taste.

We continue to learn from the master composers of the keyboard literature who were often themselves extraordinary improvisers. Now that we are creating music in our improvising, we must pursue the repertoire, studying it note by phrase by section by piece. A happy dividend is that we will play that repertory with more authority and conviction than before. We appreciate structure in a new light, having designed and worked out these forms ourselves.

Practice regularly and frequently. Begin simply. Expand boldly. Enjoy your craft as your listeners will surely enjoy your music.

A whole musical universe awaits you!

Bibliography

HYMNALS

The Baptist Hymnal. Nashville, Tenn.: The Southern Baptist Convention Press, 1991.
Great Hymns of the Faith. Grand Rapids, Mich.: Zondervan, 1968.
The New English Hymnal. Norwich, Conn.: The Canterbury Press, 1986.
The Hymnal 1982. New York: The Episcopal Church Hymnal Corporation, 1985.
Hymnbook for Christian Worship. Valley Forge, Penn. and St. Louis: The Judson Press, American Baptist Church, The Bethany Press, 1970.
Hymns Ancient and Modern. New Standard ed. Bungay, Suffolk, Eng.: Hymns Ancient and Modern, 1983.
Pilgrim Hymnal. Boston: The Pilgrim Press, 1958.
The Presbyterian Hymnal: Hymns, Psalms and Spiritual Songs. Louisville, Ky.: Westminster/John Knox Press, 1990.
The Hymnal of the United Church of Christ. Philadelphia: United Church Press, 1974.
The United Methodist Hymnal. Nashville, Tenn.: The United Methodist Publishing House, 1989.
The Lutheran Book of Worship. Minneapolis and Philadelphia: Augsburg Publishing House and the Board of Publication of the Lutheran Church in America, 1978.
With One Voice: Australian Hymnal. London: Collins Liturgical Publications, 1985.
Worship. 3d ed. Chicago: GIA Publications, 1986.

TEXTS

Here are listed but a few of many excellent textbooks which I have found most useful and practical for the student of improvisation. Again, a fluency in all these fields is essential to the improviser's success. The greater the knowledge, the greater the achievement. Please note that each of these books may be used as a reference for a specific problem as well as a general text.

Berry, Wallace. *Form in Music.* Englewood Cliffs, N.J.: Prentice-Hall, 1966.
Dupré, Marcel. *Cours complet d'improvisation à l'orgue.* 2 vols. Paris: Alphonse Leduc, 1925.
Hindemith, Paul. *Traditional Harmony.* 2 vols. Mainz: Schott, 1943, 1953.
Kennan, Kent. *Counterpoint.* 3d ed. New York: Prentice-Hall, 1987.
Piston, Walter. *Harmony.* 5th ed. New York: W.W. Norton, 1987.
Tournemire, Charles. *Précis d'exécution, de registration et d'improvisation à l'orgue.* Paris: Editions Max Eschig, 1936.

Organ Literature

Individual Composers

Bach, Johann Sebastian. *Complete Organ Works.* Kassel: Bärenreiter, 1958.
Brahms, Johannes. *Complete Organ Works.* Edited by George S. Bozarth. Munich: Henle, 1988.
Buxtehude, Dietrich. *Sämtliche Orgelwerke.* Edited by Josef Hedar. Copenhagen: Wilhelm Hansen Edition, 1952.
Distler, Hugo. *Kleine Orgelchoralbearbeitungen,* Op. 8/3. Kassel-Wilhelmshöhe: Bärenreiter, 1938.
Dupré, Marcel. *Soixante-dix-neuf Chorals,* Op. 28. New York: Gray, 1931.
———. *Trois préludes et fugues,* Op. 7. Paris: Leduc, 1920.
———. *Trois préludes et fugues,* Op. 36. Paris: Bornemann, 1940.
———. *Variations sur un Noël,* Op. 20. Paris: Leduc, 1923.
Franck, César. *Oeuvres Complètes pour Orgue.* Paris: Durand, 1859, 1868, 1878, 1884, 1892.
Karg-Elert, Sigfrid. *Chorale-Improvisations,* Op. 65. Leipzig: Breitkopf & Härtel, 1908–1940.
Mendelssohn-Bartholdy, Felix. *Complete Organ Works.* Edited by William A. Little. 5 vols. London: Novello, 1990.
Pachelbel, Johann. *Organ Works.* Edited by K. Matthaei. Vols. II and III: Chorale Preludes. Kassel-Wilhelmshöhe: Bärenreiter, 1931.
Peeters, Flor. *Hymn Preludes for the Liturgical Year.* 24 vols. New York: Peters, 1959–1966.
———. *30 Chorale Preludes.* 3 vols. New York: Peters, 1950.
Pepping, Ernst. *Zwei Choralvorspiele.* Copenhagen: Wilhelm Hansen Musik-Forlag, 1932.
———. *Zwölf Choralvorspiele.* Kassel-Wilhelmshöhe: Bärenreiter, 1957.
Reger, Max. *Choralvorspiele,* Op. 67. 3 vols. London: Hinrichsen, 1900.
———. *Dreissig Kleine Choralvorspiele,* Op. 135a. New York: Peters, 1915.
Saint-Saëns, Charles-Camille. *Six préludes et fugues.* 2 vols. Paris: Durand, 1894, 1898.
Sowerby, Leo. *Meditations on Communion Hymns.* New York: Gray, 1942.
Sweelinck, Jan Pieterszoon. *Orgelchoräle.* Kassel-Wilhelmshöhe: Bärenreiter, 1949.
Tournemire, Charles. *Cinq Improvisations.* Edited by Maurice Duruflé. Paris: Durand, 1958.
———. *L'orgue mystique.* Op. 55, 56, 57. Paris: Heugel, 1938.
Vierne, Louis. *Pièces de fantaisie,* Opp. 51, 53, 54, 55. Paris: Henry Lemoine, 1926/27.
———. *Vingt-quatre Pièces en Style Libre,* Op. 31. 2 vols. Paris: Durand, 1914.
Walcha, Helmut. *Choralvorspiele.* 3 vols. New York: Peters, 1954, 1963, 1966.

Anthologies

Alte Meister des Orgelspiels. Neue Folge. 2 vols. Edited by Karl Straube. New York: Peters, 1929.
Choralvorspiele alter Meister. Edited by Karl Straube. New York: Peters, 1951.

HYMN IMPROVISATIONS

Bairstow, Edward C. *Organ Accompaniments.* London: Oxford University Press, 1941.

Hancock, Gerre. *Organ Improvisations for Hymn Singing.* 2 vols. Chapel Hill, N.C.: Hinshaw Music, 1975, 1990.

———. *Organ Improvisations for Advent and Christmas Hymns.* Chapel Hill, N.C.: Hinshaw Music, 1991.

———. *Organ Improvisations for Lent and Easter Hymns.* Chapel Hill, N.C.: Hinshaw Music, 1994.

Noble, T. Tertius. *Fifty Free Organ Accompaniments to Well-Known Hymn Tunes.* Miami: CPP/Belwin, 1949.

———. *Free Organ Accompaniments to One Hundred Well-Known Hymn Tunes.* Miami: CPP/Belwin, 1949.